Days *of*
Wonder

BOOKS BY GRACE SCHULMAN

POETRY

Burn Down the Icons

Hemispheres

For That Day Only

The Paintings of Our Lives

Days of Wonder: New and Selected Poems

CRITICISM AND TRANSLATION

Ezra Pound

Songs of Cifar *(with Ann McCarthy de Zavala),*
by Pablo Antonio Cuadra

At the Stone of Losses: Poems by T. Carmi

Marianne Moore: The Poetry of Engagement

DAYS *of* WONDER

NEW AND SELECTED POEMS

Grace Schulman

A MARINER BOOK

Houghton Mifflin Company

BOSTON   NEW YORK

FIRST MARINER BOOKS EDITION 2003

For information about permission to reproduce selections from
this book, write to Permissions, Houghton Mifflin Company,
215 Park Avenue South, New York, New York 10003.

Visit our Web site: www.houghtonmifflinbooks.com.

Library of Congress Cataloging-in-Publication Data

Schulman, Grace.
    Days of wonder : new and selected poems / Grace Schulman.
        p. cm.
    ISBN 0-618-08623-4
    ISBN 0-618-34082-3 (pbk.)
        I. Title.

    PS3569.C538 D3 2002
    811'.54—dc21   2001039531

Book design by Anne Chalmers
Typeface: Linotype-Hell Fairfield

Printed in the United States of America

QUM 10 9 8 7 6 5 4 3 2 1

FOR JEROME L. SCHULMAN

Nu sculan herigean   heofonrices Weard,
(Now we shall praise heaven's keeper)

— Caedmon's Hymn

The lyf so shorte, the craft so long to lerne,
Th' assay so hard, so sharp the conquerynge.

— Geoffrey Chaucer,
"The Parliament of Fowles"

ACKNOWLEDGMENTS

Grateful acknowledgment is made to Sheep Meadow Press for permission to reprint poems from *For That Day Only* (1994) and from *Hemispheres* (1984), and to Princeton University Press, which published *Burn Down the Icons* (1976). An early version of that collection's title poem appeared as a pamphlet, printed by the Seafront Press, Dublin.

Poems from the earlier books first appeared, some in slightly different versions, in *American Poetry Review, Antaeus, Barrow Street, Boulevard, A Celebration for Stanley Kunitz on His Eightieth Birthday, DoubleTake, Forthcoming, Forward, Grand Street, The Hudson Review, The Humanist, The Kenyon Review, Michigan Quarterly, The Nation, New Letters, The New Republic, The New Yorker, The Ohio Review, The Paris Review, Pequod, Ploughshares, Poetry, Poetry Northwest, Prairie Schooner, Shenandoah, The Texas Observer, Theology Today, TriQuarterly Review, The Yale Review,* and *The Western Humanities Review.*

Of the new poems in this volume, "Repentance of an Art Critic, 1925" and "An Empty Surfboard on a Quiet Sea" appeared in *The Paris Review,* "Job's Question on Nevis" appeared in *TriQuarterly Review,* and "Flags," "Grandmother's Sea," and "1932" appeared in *The Sewanee Review.*

The author wishes to thank the Corporation of Yaddo, the MacDowell Colony, the Rockefeller Foundation at Bellagio, and the Karolyi Foundation, where many of these poems were written, and Baruch College, CUNY, for its continuing encouragement and support. Above all, I thank my friends.

CONTENTS

From THE PAINTINGS OF OUR LIVES (2001)

From

BURN DOWN THE ICONS

(1976)

THE ABBESS OF WHITBY

There must have been an angel at his ear
When Caedmon gathered up his praise and sang,
Trembling in a barn, of the beginning,
Startled at words he never knew were there.

I heard a voice strike thunder in the air:
Of many kings, only one god is king!
There must have been an angel at his ear
When Caedmon gathered up his praise and sang.

When Caedmon turned in fear from songs of war,
Gleemen who sang the glories of the king
And holy men wondered that so great a power
Could whirl in darkness and force up his song;
There must have been an angel at his ear
When Caedmon gathered up his praise and sang.

Whitby Abbey

Whitby Abbey rots like a skull
Where hairy horizons spin draggled
Trees. Black fragment on white sky,
Those sockets once held stained-glass eyes;
Now black birds thread white hollows.

The moors are a lunar country.
Lifeless above my head,
Hills revolve while I lose my way in craters,
Crags at false distances and
Blackface sheep. Strange swamps threaten
Less than confusion. Eyes drift skyward
(No houses, birds, flowers),
Anchored, caught in

The death's-head.
Legend or truth?
I know now
Caedmon sang here.

Written on a Road Map

This chapel stands between Morgan and Dol
Inside the gargoyle's head of Brittany
Where towns are pale gray names and roads are numbers;
Nameless, deserted; it is closed for August.

But how the shadows of a Calvary
Flicker like puppets managed by the sun;
In the yard, a soldier's name is cut on stone,
His life, in numbers, and a word, *Regrets*.

Barbara of the storm, John of the sea,
Saint Catherine fix me here, your fire my fire,
Establishing a chapel on a map
To stop the blur of trees, the flow of roads.

NAMES

"This is ozone," you said,
staring at absolute air,
startled by all things
palpable, familiar;
the less we know
about a thing, the more
names we give it.
Nominal friend,
I find you in rain,
see you in waves that radiate
rainbows,
your voice inventing
hemlocks, rose-breasted
grosbeaks. Even now,
this weedy grove spins
starflowers, arbor-
vitae, aspens,
and foamflowers
(one word);
from the bottom
of your word-hoard,
names order the world.

Horses on the Grass

From the tower window
the moon
draws a silver maple's shadow
across a spangled lawn;
                              horses
rear, manes lashing the air,
front legs floating.
                      Half monarch,
half shadow, the tree
aspires to the sky;
one branch, cracked by lightning,
scrapes the earth.
                      Reflected
on the grass, bent twigs
are curved hooves, galloping
as the moon rises.

Divided it stands
in wholeness, mourning
its victories, praising
the god of trees, the king of horses.

The tree holds souls
in a bark prison
poised like a runner at the starting line —
and bolts free, wildly
pawing the ground those roots lie under.

THAT MAPLE

You are right, that maple ruined
the landscape; it was out of place.
How it stood in the middle of things,
hunched on the lawn screening
a marble nymph, her raised arms
making circles in water.
Out of the far reach of the eye
I never saw its branches; eyes rose over them
to mountains, painting images
on spindly twigs.

          You know trees
as they are; I gave one leaves
and dressed it in gold
like a love. I remember
a musical wind,
the crash-on-crash
of thunder; I never saw
lightning vein sky silver
and crack a branch
that lashed the lawn
and tracked earth
like the heart.

STREET DANCE IN BARCELONA

Alone, I watched the solemn dance begin,
Waking from a silence that deceives,
That turns footsteps, or the rustle of dry leaves
Into the clatter of a tambourine.

Their voices had been rattling that day,
Rapid as drumbeats, in the Catalan,
But a wilderness of hands reached toward the sun
Like wheatstalks risen from a ground of clay.

The crowd broke into perfect wheels, turning
To the stuttering of a wooden horn,
Quickened by the beating of the sun;
I had seen their angry faces burning.

Strangers, we stand alone but turn together
As vanes become a windmill in the wind;
One hand opens for another hand,
The wheel breaks only to include another.

Surely as Certainty Changes

Surely as certainty changes,
As tide moves sand,
As heat sends wind to force the sea into waves,
As water rises and returns in rain
Or circles into smoke and falls in vapor,
You are enchanted for you enter change
And change is holy.

As earth's weight compresses rocks
Under trees over time, you enter change,
I know your face gives light as I know fire
Alters everything,
And falls rising,
Feeds and nourishes, opens and closes.

I pray to Proteus, the god of change
And proteolysis, "the end of change
Changing in the end,"
To break old images and make you new
As love is its own effect unendingly.

THE OTHER SIDE OF HUMANKIND

For COUNTESS CATHERINE KAROLYI, VENCE

These are the hills of healed divisions;
The river we cannot see sings us awake,
Parting the mountains. I am familiar
With trees at false distances
In the clear air.

Remembering maps whose boundaries
Were scars, stitches
Of broken lines,
We grow whole—a continent
Of one color.

Twisted oaks hide
A rectangle reading,
In lapsed letters,
Chasse Interdite,
And all roads lead
To the sign
That cannot be seen.

Here, the river swims us;
We shine at moons.
Clouds whiten dark skies,
Light rings horizons after nightfall
That never seems to fall;
An ancient olive branch screens
Older stars.

Exiles, we have crossed
The solid white line
Between countries and loves
And torn selves,
Losing borders,
Questioning frontiers.

But see! Limestone terraces
Are a wall of skulls
That part like seas when you climb them,
Revealing trees,

And you stand
On your stone balcony
Framed in your chancel window,
Commanding even shadows to shed their provinces
And nightingales to sing beyond confusion.

POETRY EDITOR

Caught on a traffic island
in Park Avenue, I waited,
staring at dahlias,
cars enclosing me in a moving
parenthesis, red lights
arresting me. The stranger came,
wary, lizardlike, observing me
observe him, pressing pages
in my hand: "I want to talk with you
about matters of interest
to both — my poetry."
                          "Of course."

From a drawer with grooves
for silver needles, my dentist
reached for metaphors.
                          "Oh yes,
of course."

                  And when my neighbor
at a farmhouse in the pines
lodged notes he thought I had not seen
beneath my breakfast plate, I said again,
"Of course."

Day of Atonement: in the house of God
trumpets began an elusive,
uncertain staccato flourish;
then, the horn stuttered
that once woke me

to song: "Let mountains rise
to trumpets throughout the land."
Trembling to that blare, I saw
a choir angel flutter
a white arm that implored me
to hear his cadences.
Wavering, I whispered,
"Of course."

         And yet again
of course. For, day by day, those images
rise like smoke, turn like a windmill,
furnish a beehive
I have not arranged; I never know
when fire in some unlikely place
will seize me; when my ears will reel
to that elusive music.

         Worn at last,
I flew to Antibes and, one day,
swimming toward me
under a snorkel,
a masked man cried *"Attends!"*
his manuscript translated
into English, lying
on black stones.

         "Bien sûr," I said,
as on the traffic island.
I, too, look for mail.
And when green signals tell me to, I cross

Park Avenue,
waiting for a comet
to flare suddenly,
firing
my landscape
of bricks and glass.

The Examination:
Remembrance of Words Lost

—What happened at your orals, Grace?
Taking a pipe from a row of suckling pigs, the chairman swung
In his chair. An A-shaped face, kind voice. Eyes, rubber stamps:
Failure. Special case.

                    —I lose it now,
But I will try to call it back. Dim stars
That fade to a stare can shine at a backward glance.

—Why did you fail?

                    —I did not. Words failed *me*
When I heard words about words, and swallowed tides
Of questions, as rock-hollows suck sea.

—Why are you here?

                    —A star once summoned me,
As gravity pulls others to the ground.
That star is light-years distant from me now,
But still it burns, unseen, waiting to shine.
I wait for syllables to fall. Or burn, like ice.

—Good answer, though your style is hard to follow.
Have you tried aeronautics? Astrophysics?
These numbers: Ninety percent of you are brainless,
My records show, though eighty-six percent
Pass on the second try. But you—good teacher,
Student, lover of words. What happened, Grace?

—They led me to a room with a womb-shaped table
On which my fathers laid twelve hands. Six scraped faces nodded.
Above, fluorescent rectangles were frozen lakes
Of corrugated glass. The walls were soundproof.
I greeted a darning-egg.

                              —We haven't met
Officially.

            Mist fell. Tide went over me.

—In eighteen-eighty, where would you buy a book?

—At the corner of Third and Bleecker, in ribs of sun,
Where I left my mind.

                  Their voices bonged
Contrapuntally:

                  —The chicken or Emily Dickinson?
The egg enjoined. Another:

                        —Stephen or Hart?
Henry or William? I did not know
Which of his heads to answer. Totem pole
of painted masks gone white.

A man with a face like a dime on edge said,
Fields away,

—Was there a real
House in Albany? His headlights caught my eyes.

There was. I lived there once. But I can't recall
Where Henry was when William was at Harvard.

Their voices thrummed:

                          —Internal evidence?

                                            —Any sex
In Sextus Propertius?

                    —Elders, let me finish
Bathing. I am no exhibitionist.

When Caedmon turned from song to sing
Hild made him monk, but only after
God made him poet—and I think his God
Was some dark fierce power that forced up his song.
I cannot tell you how he sang, how syllables
Danced from a man who could not read.

                              —A monk?
Oh, yes. Of course. But nowadays we can't
Give Ph.D.s for *that*. What's your profession?

—Poet.

      —Published poet?

           —Yes.

                —Well, *poetry*
Has nothing to *do* with scholarship. Your sentence:
A year of failure and a crown of silence.

Five fathers vanished. One remained.

                  —My friend,
I see you have been walking under water.
Look upward now.

              I surfaced then, saw shadows
That had been knives, and moved into myself.

In the Country of Urgency, There Is a Language

To Marianne Moore

> *"Ezra Pound said never, NEVER to use
> any word you would not actually say in
> moments of utmost urgency."*

I

"Can you hear me? I talk slowly now,"
you said, months past. "When Ezra Pound
Came, he could not say a word."
When your voice waned, I prodded syllables,
Examined frequencies, listened for cadences,
Demanding clarity. Sounds inconceivable
Have meaning now. Four heavy stresses:
"How is your work?" Light syllables:
"Do I look well?" Fire-forced speech
Caught, wordless. It will suffice.

2

December 22, 1970

In the country of urgency, there is a language
I hear as I follow the fall of your hand
and a blue light from the door of your dark apartment.
Your body vanishes behind bedrails.
Your hand I can't let go flows into me.

Blue eyes burn images in me. Those images,
Those sounds, those necessary gestures
Are a language. They will suffice.

20

3

No note from you. Remembering your leopard,
"Spotted underneath and on its toes,"
And how you'd said, "a leopard isn't spotted
Underneath, but in the tapestries it is,
And I liked the idea," I brought the photograph
Of leopards spotted everywhere. Home from the hospital,
Immobile, in a billowing blue gown,
You stalked those beasts and raised yourself in bed:
"Those are cheetahs, Grace!" and lay down again.

4

Your silence is a terrible fire in me that sings on to be fed,
A musical wind that splits my craft, hail-hard, that lashes me
     dumb.
It is a strange country. Where are the maps,
The lighthouses, the gyroscope you gave me
That rights itself in motion? I have forgotten my name
As well as the irregular conjugations I memorized.
Occasionally, though, a blue light flashes directions
Over dangerous shale, and I hear you
Over protest shouts, explosions, immolations,
Over unreliable telephone connections, I hear you
Over labels, over a broken air conditioner, a plane;
I hear you over the silences we call conversation.
Your voice rolls in me thunder in a night of invisible stars,
And I wake to the sounds of your silence. They are a language.
          They will suffice.

Birds on a Blighted Tree

Free things are magnets to the moving eye,
Beckoning the mind to rouse the dead;
Under a cloud's passing power
A spire sails — a mast.
These birds antagonize a tree:
Scavengers invade decay,
Winter's engraved in air.
Defiantly they strain for light and fly,
Tightening branches to bows.
Iconoclasts impress indelible
Veronicas on living things,
Leaving a branch leafless.
Free things breed freedom;
That dead arm beating.

EPITHALAMION

Look there! *The Lovers*
In the Flowers.
Chagall's lovers, forever
Ungoverned by gravity,
Surface the air
Like water, or
Lean on lilacs
Above a moon,
Over the distant
Fragment of a castle.
Is it fantasy? Hands,
Faces, arms
Are real, but made
Of smoke: sometimes,
In wind,
It skims the earth
But always rises.

SPAIN, 1964

Green lights grow from the trees in San Sebastian
To make the poplars greener than they are;
Along the waterfront, loudspeakers blare
March cadences just as the night comes on.

Voices contend the warlike sound, but slowly
Speech flickers and dies, and heels obey;
Anger: flame quivers to survive the wind
As music drowns the sea and stills the mind.

This harbor's outsize arms contain the sea;
An Eden of green trees across the bay
Is an artifice of light. Such things compel
The burning eye as drums enclose the will.

We watch the pantomime of waves like thought
Made visible; we hear but do not hear
Voices go under the mutter of unseen trumpets.
The news is edited of wars; the air

Clean as these white streets. Waves gathering thunder
In silence, our mute voices fill with anger
Now and until the sun burns through these trees
And birds disturb the air with free, imperfect cries.

BURIAL OF A FISHERMAN IN HYDRA

The day time failed began as usual.
Seeing the sun strike mica on the rocks,
I raced down terraces, past white
Sea houses casting black trapezoids
To watch the nightboat stagger in.
No nightboat, but a strange gray cutter
Moved into the harbor, bringing a fisherman
Who died in Athens, in a hospital.
There was a priest, a brilliant procession
Balancing scalloped crosses; the bells
Wailed; his women were black birds
Ridding the pier of swimmers and fishermen.
Suddenly, as though we knew him well,
The people stood in a silent chorus
Until the last cross-bearer disappeared
Among the listed saint-heads in the chapel.
Shadows that had been knives on the ground
Grew as on a sundial, measuring
The light; we followed in suppliance,
Night crowding every gutter of the rock.
In another time we might have mourned
Fallen heroes carried in from sea,
But in the imagination of the living
The fall from glory is the fall from being.
Night comes; that is the mystery of day.

Recovery

Recovery: returning
to the village where forests
are spirals of fire, to climb
narrow roads and find that pine
torn by lightning, its branches holding
stars of needles that strain the sky,
pointing upward, stiff
as hands in prayer.

To return in silence; I have touched
the nightingale I cannot see,
crossing the river
that drives through rocks
and sings in my blood,
treasure of my being.

I remember how the surgeon smiled, masked
in green gauze. I woke to eyes
watching me through lenses; voices
saying it was over, murmuring
"Recover."

Here I rise
with the mountains.
I have given my name
and my language
to the primitive saints
in the chapel. I live in their light

and see the faces of all people
as one face.

Love, there is a world of pain
where sun fires bricks and glass
slowly as a season. I cherish pain
for it stills the sky to a halt,
arresting night.
Here may I see
those shadows stagger
that etch the olive,
recover,
follow a sun that makes days
green as the beginning,
light as creation;
let the river return things whole
in exchange for what has been broken.

Burn Down the Icons

What happened to Cassandra? She who cried
In me "Love is war!" has died, loving.
And Daphne, whose flesh grew leaves?
Breasts now, and twig-shaped nerves.
Father, forgive me. It had to be.
I never promised to be Saint Veronica
When you pressed images on me, printed in blood
On a white scarf. Or when you carved me in marble,
And gazed into the dry wells of my eyes,
Did you think I would not dissolve?

Well, burn down the icons. I have moved
Out of the Prado. Your best fresco
Cracks from the ceiling. I have gone
Beyond my body, five feet eleven and three-quarters
Inches of tangled philodendron. I am water.

Call out the curia. Unsanctify me.
Erase my feast day from the calendar.
Shatter the stained-glass windows of my mind.
They were idolaters who cut the palm,
Two anchors and an arrow on my tomb
Found in the catacombs. I am no martyr.

Love was my habit. I know my heart moved trees.
Love called my eyes to change things of this world.
But I did not believe it. And how could I persuade you
That those visions you admired were astigmatism.

Makers of images, what you created in me
I was. But see me new! My nipples are cathedrals,
My flesh is a miracle. I flow to the ocean
Where all the rivers of the earth come together.
My body is a holy vessel. I am fire and air.

Do not desert me now, although I pray
To a genital god, and have let blaze
Strange images, my means of transportation.
I have established my chapel in water.
I would move through mountains. But fathers,
Let me return to a safe harbor; like the waves'
Slate-sheets, crash in the jetties of your arms.

Moon

Having no fire of my own, I shine
But never burn. I receive the light.
Man and woman, I gather both
Inside of me, surviving darkness,
Changing to grow whole
Or starving
Into halves and quarters.
If I do not feed flames,
Transparent fragments linger
After daybreak,
And for brief moments
I cover the sun.

LETTER TO HELEN

For DR. HELENA WALDMAN-GOLD, 1898–1943

I

Your face broods from a sepia photograph:
Eyes light over cheekbones.
Helen, I cannot lose your indelible
name, although I lose
others of the time.
When acts burn, there are images,
icons of blood and sweat
printed on my mind.

I have to recreate
your deed from rumors
in the quick ears
of the child I was, from Black Books
I was allowed *not* to read. I have to guess
you knew our law of invisible
light: "Therefore choose life
that thou and thy seed shall live."
We dance to songs
in a world below ice, below time,
sleepwalk to laws
that manage our acts. Living our law
and science, your faith,
condemned to die,
you leaped from a tower in Poland, your death
firing our lives.

2

For years I would lessen your nobility,
call it impulsive, plead
it was useless, say
the sudden splendid act is no great thing,
survival is; the steady patient choice
of rightness over time, and excellence —
patience, the hero's passion.

To yield is to come back, I said, as water
yields to cleave stone, as tide ebbs
to move shorelines. Awakening at last
in a strange country, sun-dazed, I knew
the world's calm when acts
are stilled. Storms coned inward,
I stared down wind that spirals to an eye,
and knew I was the heart of the storm,
born of the same that war is born.
"Therefore choose life," I cried, for David wept
when Absalom was slain, his criminal,
his outlaw son, however hard
the king had danced before God,
the ark safe in Jerusalem.

3

A transatlantic call, beamed from a satellite:
I asked him, "Will you say
Celan's *'Fadensonnen'*? I cannot find
your version." Static then,
and speech with echoes: "'there are
still songs to be sung ... sung ... sung ...
on the far side
of mankind ... kind ... kind.'
Damn that echo!"
My friend, your quiet voice insists on peace,
like "Dona Nobis Pacem," in an antiphonal
high mass with fuguelike shadows.

4

Blood forces up my praise.
I am a fountain, juggling blades
to God, while everywhere the dead
lie on the streets, in crevasses, in fields;
today a woman set herself on fire,
her body charred, her flesh burned to a log,
fire flattened her mouth and slit her eyes.

Fire forces me. I shout my praise
to the other side of humankind,
my name a blue number burned
on forearms of the imagination.
Your name was, is, will be, Helen.

And you will come for years, salamander,
name of fire and unharmed by fire.
That is what icons are, indelible
prints on the mind. Your image is a fresco
that will not come down
in dust. Because you lived your life I shine
in flames, burning but not consumed,
changing to be myself, as though if water burned
it would be water all the more.
Courage you gave me, Helen, and your name
draws me like fire.

From

HEMISPHERES

(1984)

BLESSED IS THE LIGHT

Blessed is the light that turns to fire, and blessed the flames
      fire makes of what it burns.
Blessed the inexhaustible sun, for it feeds the moon that shines
      but does not burn.
Praised be hot vapors in earth's crust, for they force up
        mountains that explode as molten rock and cool, like love
        remembered.
Holy is the sun that strikes the sea, for surely as water burns,
        life and death are one. Holy the sun, maker of change, as
        it melts ice into water that lessens mountains, hones peaks,
        and carves gullies.
Sacred is the mountain that crumbles over time. Jagged peaks
        promise permanence but change, planed by rock slides, cut
        by avalanche, crushed, eroded, leached of minerals.
Behold the arcs your eyes make when you speak. Behold the hands,
        white fire. Branches of pine, holding votive candles, they
        command, disturbed by wind, the fire that sings in me.
Blessed is whatever alters, turns, revolves, just as the gods
      move when the mind moves them.
Praised be the body, our bodies, that lie down and open and
      rise, falling in flame.

CITY OF MANY NAMES

Jerusalem, meaning "holy," is unholy.
The morning sun strikes stone walls bone and amber,
turns a black cone ocherous at noon,
and cuts new shadows slate gray, olive green.
A gold and a silver cupola seem stationary,
but change like the sun and moon: the Dome of the Rock
swells and inflames Al-Aqsa. Nothing is stable.

Jerusalem, meaning "whole," has been divided
by roads, lines, streets that alter with each war.
The Old City's in quarters behind battlements.
The cannon shot of Ramadan explodes
above the Western Wall, where men and women
whisper to what's unseen behind the wall.

Loudspeakers blare muezzin chants and drown
church bells, sabbath prayers. The local music:
shellbursts, sonic booms, and people's voices,
clear as birds. Unfounded city. Fallen,
everything rises: Mary flies to heaven;
Muhammad gallops skyward on a horse;
flames curl to many gods. In this dark chapel,
the Copts intone, and nearby, Ethiopians
sing praises, while a man rests on his hands
and knees, face to the ground, under black icons.

Borders that terrify have summoned me
to cancel edges, nullify horizons;
mirrors of my mind transform divisions.
I climbed a winding road and discovered seas
in air; waves silver hills, their cadences
winds seething through trees, partitions gone.
It was a miracle, or an illusion:
when I walked down, the boundaries reappeared.

Yet cypresses that vanish are still there.
At night this soldier's name cut in white stone
is gone; salamanders with snowflake feet
turn oat-colored and orange on the terrace.
Even the stone walls waver behind acacias.
Jerusalem has shadows that recede
in spangling sun as tide effaces seamarks.
I live for what I never have believed.

LET THERE BE TRANSLATORS!

*And the Lord said, "Behold, the people is one and they have all
one language ... Go to, let us go down, and there confuse their
language, that they may not understand one another's speech."*

—Genesis XI: 6, 7.

When God confused our languages, he uttered,
in sapphire tones: "Let there be translators!"
And there were conjurors and necromancers
and alchemists, but they did not suffice:
they turned trees into emeralds, pools to seas.

God spoke again: "Let there be carpenters
who fasten edges, caulk the seams, splice timbers."
They were good.
                God said: "Blessed is the builder
who leaves his tower, turns from bricks and mortar
to marvel at the flames, the smith who fumbles
for prongs, wields andirons, and prods live coals,
who stokes the hearth and welds two irons as one."

Praised was the man who wrote his name in other
handwriting, who spoke in other tones,
who, knowing elms, imagined ceiba trees
and cypresses as though they were his own,
finding new music in each limitation.

Holy the one who lost his speech to others,
subdued his pen, resigned his failing sight
to change through fire's change, until he saw
earth's own fire, the radiant rock of words.

Sutton Hoo Ship Burial

In the British Museum are objects belonging to a seventh-cen-
tury Anglo-Saxon king, which were found in August 1939 in the
remains of a boat at Sutton Hoo, on Suffolk's River Deben, near
the North Sea.

He rose out of the sea, the last warrior,
months before Dunkirk, days before invasion,
not his remains, but things: a boar's-head brooch;
epaulets, coins; a six-stringed willow harp;
christening spoons beside an aurochs horn.
His helmet found, the absent king endured,
his house battered by water; and as water

turns to ice and kills, it broke the hull,
scattering narrow strakes that marked the sand,
nailprints; but the hull would give life back again
as snails plunge into earth before the spring—
a resurrection shell; so he appeared,
beached among swampferns fronded in the bog,
monarch of nests and ruler of enclosures.

He may have been the real Beowulf,
beekeeper, guardian of law. He fought nightmares,
not men: he conquered trolls and firedragons
and slew Cain's sons, sea monsters, keeping peace
within himself, dreading the heart's Grendels
that brought invaders, past and future wars,
Danelaw that split the kingdom, killing men.

Weeks before lightning war, and the sea blockades,
a woman found the last warrior's bark;
his body lay in heath covered by bracken.

A pagan ship, a Christian burial
in holy ground for a king who sanctified
God and the gods. Not his remains but things
would sail him to the next world as a king.

Ring-giver, father of swords, of artisans,
emerging, moving toward me in the night,
he brings me dreams of refuge in a shell.
I see his shadow now, for I hear my past
in my body's shell, in reveries of almonds.
As he loomed out of the sea to tell his story
of mud-drenched creatures in the mind's black waters

who thrashed ungoverned ghosts at the sea's edge,
I find my house in a stone, my world in acorns,
my solitude in galleys holding bowls,
bronze stags, gold buckles, swords inlaid with garnets,
stars locked in hollows, hidden and revealed.
In rocks I will know eels and sea-anemones
before I surface into murderous air.

Songs of My Fathers

Schmuel, my grandmother's grandfather, came from Romania with the Homestead Act of 1862 to Garden City, Kansas, where he sold steam tractors and farm machines.

Sliding a skullcap under a wide-brimmed hat,
he wore a Star of David and a sheriff's badge,
had sideburns and a beard, and carried guns.
Even in those fields, he guarded law,

David before the Ark, shouting thanksgiving.
His sons went east to marry in the faith,
and all returned except my ancestor,
Zavel, who fathered cantors and lawyers.

"What is the faith?" I asked my grandmother,
who smiled and closed her book, *The Range of Reason.*
"It is tenacity. The will to live. To sing."
To sing. To chant. To change: cantors, *cantare.*

Now I imagine others who remained,
farmers in Kansas, dancing to old laws
they cannot name. On holy nights, they leave
chairs vacant, never dreaming of Elijah.

Sometimes they drink wine from silver cups,
singing like sea wind, savage joy and pain
grown into thunder. They never question
why, from where, that perilous song has come.

Hemispheres

Our bodies, lucent under the bedclothes,
fit tightly like the pieces of a broken
terra-cotta vase now newly mended,
smooth surfaces, no jagged edges visible.

I've read that countries were so interlocked
before tectonic heavings, when the ocean
parted Mexico and Mauritania.
Brazil's shoulder was hoisted to Nigeria,
Italy pressed Libya, Alaska
lay so close to Russia that fingers touched.
Our tremulous hands held fast in sleep at dawn;
legs, arms entwined, one continent, one mass.

EASY AS WIND

Easy as wind that lifts white pine
and blows for flowers, showering rose
petals on cold marble statues,
we touch and separate.
                                        I am familiar
with water burning the land,
turning catbrier to red-brown wire,
clinging to live. I have seen flame
waiting to burn, altering shadows,
striking rectangles beyond the trees.
Even the sea collects its powers and strikes,
baffling the sand's composure.
                                        But now, suddenly,
wherever I look I see wind
I cannot see, touching nowhere, everywhere.

MORNING SONG

Norwegian spruce trees, veering to red-brown.
You are asleep, your body cool as dawn.
As I turn to leave, sun strikes the terrace,
affirming day. Amazed, through junipers,
my eyes raise watchmen on the mansion tower.
Our clothes will spin together in the laundromat:
doomed lovers circle, drifting on the winds.

LOSSES

Life's gains are losses: water leaches rock,
rivers erode and deltas restore the land;
the sun melts ice, turns rain to clouds of mist.
Wind that spins palms in circles like propellers
squanders its force; the fire that feeds destroys.

Each morning burns what night had bound together,
waking us, amazed, staring in wonder,
broken apart. So for all things refused,
I turn, as ships spill wind to change their course:
just as the sea recedes, I grow with loss.

THE STARS AND THE MOON

In Legends of the Jews, *Lewis Ginzberg writes that an Egyptian princess hung a tapestry woven with diamonds and pearls above King Solomon's bed. When the king wanted to rise, he thought he saw stars and, believing it was night, slept on.*

Scaling ladders with buckets of white enamel,
I painted the stars and the moon on my windowpanes
to hold back days and nights. I yanked the telephone
and stopped the wooden clock. The weeks a lightning stroke,
desire turned to love. With my blue diamond,
I sliced minutes in half and made days vanish,
fooling the hours.

           I became so skillful
at firmaments that miracles occurred:
a bearded comet moved across the room
breeding no omens, tearing no major kingdoms
into small provinces, but there it was,
reminding us that rock may spin and flare,
lifting the senses, burning into sight.

You eased pale hands away; I saw your shoulders
recede through doorways, watched your image fail
with your famished smile. I left our room
with dream-filled eyes, and standing in the sun,
I gazed at bricks and glass and saw, suddenly,
flashing in stony light, the stars and the moon.

THE MESSENGER

I would have been surprised, but I had seen him
halting at daybreak, hovering around,
plowing a sky half dark with stars, half mauve
with iridescent clouds, then watched him circle
and glide through buckled windowpanes to say:

"I am a superior Hebrew angel.
I have one thousand eyes and many wings."
"Don't give me angels," I said, seeing the cherub
standing vigil, writing what I said
in monolithic letters in a register,
plummet, shout his praise, and rearrange
layers of wings.

              I glanced at your chair,
saw how the bed assumed your body's form,
recalled how, mouth on mouth, we slept, and how
your hands were lightning spears.

                     You went away.
How could I know that I would sign my name
as yours, that I would hear your words
as miracles and question other vows
for your laws, written in white fire.

It was that angel, made of air and wind,
who caused it all. Beyond the angel,
sun that never brightens, never fades.

THE FLIGHT

That day I hired a private detective to follow me,
and could not read his notes. In a tangled grove,
I hid behind white pines, compressed my body,
then watched him write, left-handed and myopic,
under an Irish cap, when I asked for help
from strangers who spoke Slavic languages.
Wary, moving ahead, I found a depot,
watched an immense train churn, haloed in steam,
and boarded, second class. I had no ticket,
and my expired passport represented
a drooping head with unfamiliar eyes.
Unshaken, rows behind, the stranger waited,
wielding camera and pen. Across the border
I disembarked, but knew he would capture me,
with soundless footsteps, even on black gravel.

I tried to recall my crime. I know I am guilty,
but never why. Lawless, I have ignored
those signs: WRONG WAY; GO BACK and NO WAY OUT,
circles that tell me YOU ARE HERE. I gather
it is the whispers that explode, the looks
that make dogs whimper. When I bow in prayer
I think of love; I know I've killed my friends,
pelting them with a touch—and yet I've heard
they are alive. Besides, that's not the real

offense. I would cross any path, or trek
through swamps to find my crime. But even he,
that bald, insistent man who follows me,
unsleeping, cannot tell me what I've done.

IMAGES OF GRAVITY

1

Buoyancy:
the wind moves
a swamp reed
that the finch rides.

2

Force:
swallows
plummet like hail,
careening
over wild roses.

3

Vector:
bulrushes
gesture in wind,
dancer's arms.

4

Density:
gulls,
angular in flight,
stand potbellied.

5

Weightlessness:
I've heard the albatross

sleeps on the wing
in the heart of a storm,
gliding
on currents it raises.

6

Acceleration:
dead
birds
fall
fast.

7

Balance:
fragile as a grasshopper,
my house stands
on spindly pilings.

8

Momentum:
waves crash
still rising
in vapor.

THE MARSH

For years nothing grew
in acid soil
near my house
that stood on scant legs.
Then, year by year, I saw
shadblow trees,
and creepers that curled around
their striated bark.
When fires of wind and water
burned the marsh,
only bare vines
hooked into trees
survived,
as we had, joined
together, in the house
on bulldozed sandy ground,
draggled, storm-blown,
still holding fast
to memories of dense vines
as if we knew life's law
was cleave or die.

SMALL METEOR

As comets go, it was a disappointment.
However perilously close to earth
it circled, still it wreaked no tidal waves,
fired no earthquakes, demons, or disasters.
Astronomers predicted blazing flight,
then blinked at its arrival. You could hardly
see it in darkness, let alone by day,
before it dwindled. Only the tireless few
saw it after sundown, with binoculars.

Still, that shooting star, thrust into space,
recalled that rock may burn suddenly, spin
for centuries before it shines, and rise
falling, surviving night.
                              I told my friend
about the paltry star, and he shook loose
from memory the comet of 1910,
screened through smoked glass. When I saw his eyes
go gray, I knew how anything alive
may flare, shine, and survive. Small star: small miracle.

Instructions for a Journey

There are no provisions, but your guide
may teach you hymns during the long flight.
Sing lauds and benedictions on all nights
to soothe the guards of houses, one inside

the other. Take your journal, and a pen,
staplers, and dictionaries when you travel.
The landscape may appear unusual:
gray birds sail low; birches are frozen bones.

Prepare to see men seventy miles high,
their shoulders parasangs apart, with many heads
and tongues. All measurements are odd. Their eyes
flash lightning. Then the terror, as your body

assumes new forms, abandoning old molds.
First Heaven: Go through Customs and Security.
You'll see blunt hills the color of chalcedony.
Igneous water flows in riverbeds.

Chapels have stained-glass windows cut in moonstone,
marked "war" and "peace." Angels who pacify
the world praise God; they are condemned to die
if they sing louder than men, or out of tune.

In Sixth Heaven, angels of wrath and silence
greet you. Cherubs and seraphim dance;
gazelles with dappled faces flank the throne;
light strikes the trembling heart. You are alone.

You'll see a god of fire trailing stars,
then climb to see the chariot throne, and still
survive unharmed. Through blinding flame, through water,
you'll enter seven heavens and fall, whole.

From

FOR THAT DAY ONLY

(1994)

FOR THAT DAY ONLY

NEW YORK, JUNE 11, 1883

Daybreak, and she left her poppyseed roll
to follow them as they walked through the city
carrying the dead child, her fourth brother

born in their new world. Sunlight revealed
a stark, unbending man; a hawklike woman
in a stiff wig, wearing a nubby shawl;

and Uncle Ben, with the bouncing silver watch,
their only kin. Now they exhausted sorrow
by humming sacred phrases in the trek

from Grand Street to the Brooklyn cemetery.
Her mother glanced at her, the oldest daughter,
who had rocked beside the stove and read to him

English words that rang like bits of praise
fallen out of prayer, from Homer's tales
of a nymph whose breath filled sails, images

a storyteller scooped out of a basket
that pierced the morning fog, then disappeared,
like a cat's firecoal eyes—alive, but never

as real as asphalt on this long day.
She never saw the film inside his throat,
and had to be pried away when she tried to breathe

life into his mouth. Just before dawn,
she saw their forms as she sang to the baby's pillow;
hands stroked her hand and led her to the march.

And now, how bright they were. How ... well, how *visible*.
How steep her father's shoulders. The same light
that warmed them froze gray towers in what was

her first view of the city beyond the neighborhood,
beyond the block. Seeing everything,
trying to see nothing at either side,

she almost smiled at trees, jerked back her head,
remembering herself, and hid her eyes
when she saw a woman speed a bicycle

as though about to rise up over the pavement
like a streetcar's horses that, though ponderous,
might break into a gallop in the wind.

Circles bloomed everywhere: a yellow ball
flew at a hedge; coaches had creaky wheels;
a white hoop, tapped with a stick, zoomed from behind.

There was a brown house with a tulip patch,
for just one family—or so a brass-star
policeman said, who ushered them through crowds

in City Hall Park, and waved at flags on buildings
with plate-glass shop windows. She tripped on loose
cobblestones, and where the streets were roads,

the ground marsh after a night of rain,
she danced and fell, her ankle boots soaked through,
then clambered to the walk to watch a beetle

scurry toward some weeds grown through black gaps
in concrete rectangles. She tried to touch
the statue of a man in bronze that was mottled,

green-going-black, with a beckoning,
historical hand, creased at its great wrist.
Longing to stop by a straw-hat cart near a girl

who tugged at a hatless woman with red real hair,
she pushed on to the harbor, where a gull
barely skimmed her head, and climbed the new

Brooklyn Bridge, her alley to the dead.
Chanting lines of the Psalms to secular tunes
that moved her—local streetcries, arias—

she studied the bearded man in front of her,
observed his set jaw, stirred to his praise,
and feared the tiny boy would grow as heavy

as a bag of stones by the time their journey ended.
Stalwart, proud, he held their grief to his chest
for that day only; moments after sunrise

her mother had raised white arms and yielded up
the shapeless sack. Sun growing higher,
she knew that she, the oldest daughter,

would haul that ragged body even after
the procession ended, when they returned
by gaslight to their dim rooms, and, in fact,

whenever she walked alone in her new city —
brick-hard and vast, but never unredeeming —
the next day and the next one and the next.

The Present Perfect

I saw the cells on TV, as they swam
up to the egg, tails lashing, and I heard
the wind-tunnel sound they make, the steady hum

of thousands, blind, threadlike, worn, but soaring
through waterfalls in their drive to live, move,
and set the egg revolving like a star.

For us, there was no miracle of birth.
No genes, no geniuses. And yet, okay,
we had other things: our work, our history

scrawled on Margaux labels and libretti,
and, after all, no cribs, no sticky plums,
no pulling paper napkins one by one

from a metal box, to mop up dumped ice cream.
But then again, no immortality:
in my religion, children to speak my name

after I am. No heir to your kindness,
your skill with a kite, your father's whimsy,
or to my mother's mother's diamond pin.

And yet we had each other's silences;
freedom to wander with no fixed plan,
now fixed in photos of sylphs that resemble us,

peering down cliffs in Brittany at ragged boards
floated up from dinghies lost at sea,
searching for fish carved into chapels' altars,

spending our suns like out-of-date coins,
until we reached the present-perfect tense—
that have-been state where past and future merge:

we have been married thirty-four years.
I see the kids we were frisk on this lawn
in the late afternoon's unnamable light.

Too late for them, and for their unborn kids,
but not too late for us, here among cedars,
to praise the fires in rose petals on slate;

white rhododendrons, a fountain's rainbow.
I see the dot of you, meadows away,
that grows in sight as you pedal home;

your reddish hair and beard, now tarnished silver,
that once we wanted for a chromosome;
your silhouette in a Manet-like straw hat

as you bless your new astilbe: "Live and be well,"
casting aside your customary questions
for an irrational faith the plant will grow;

I hear your voice that calls me to see wildflowers
poking through gravel cracks in our neighbors' driveway,
slender but fortunate, built to last their day.

AFTER THE DIVISION

Here it is! In an unbleached photograph,
Plato's two halves of man-and-woman, cast
of our shadows, sliced and joined again: four arms,
four legs, two heads. Metallic, silver-gray,

that blade clicks from our feet at acute angles
from our bodies, then it becomes a gaunt,
barbarous giant and creeps toward the sea.
Below us, in the foreground, the white sand

is ruffled now by footsole indentations,
and you, above the tracks, a leggy matador,
brandish a towel the sun has gored blood red.
You search the land; musing behind your shoulder,

I watch the ocean. After that sun fell,
we cracked apart. I listened for your silences
in clamorous voices; looked for your merest
accidental glance among the usual

predators. With quartz-clear eyes
you told me I looked lovely in a torn
dress, but questioned natural laws. Remember
the night you challenged probability,

tossing a coin to count one hundred heads
until the dawn, an enterprise that lulled
me but held you fast. You never pondered
gravity, compelled instead by bonds

between revolving worlds and fallen apples.
Driven by what anemones are made of,
not by their names, calmly you insisted
that viruses have viruses, and cells

have dictionaries, and even memories.
With quiet fortitude and dour tenacity,
probing a cloud, examining a dahlia,
godless, you led me to my God. One day,

in solitude, I caught your stalky form
jackknifed over a lean golden retriever,
and avenues spun like planets. There was time.
One night I watched El Greco's cardinal

sprout your weedy beard. Still, there was time.
Unlike Dante's damned, who see the future
but not the past, I reel in what there was,
and wish when we had marched on brittle leaves

to "L'Internationale" that shadows drawn
into our forms at noon were visible.
Tonight we walk under the same mimosa trees
and wonder why we severed then; creepers

hooked into oaks to live, we held too fast,
when earth and sun — all things, irregular —
converge and separate. We ask again
why we merged to want this moment now,

and see only the creature in the photograph
(though whether it has life, as you would say,
is philosophical, depending on
degrees of selfhood), but, in any case,

a being, torn in two, grown whole, the root
our bodies spring from, moves discreetly
toward the sea. After twelve years apart,
I watch its steely edges cut the sand

and know it will glide, unseen, even when day
concludes. I wake with you and feel the sun
invent one shadow that starts out from us,
and know the time has come to begin our lives.

FOOTSTEPS ON LOWER BROADWAY

Grace Church's steeple still fishes the sky
over Broadway, and bobs up from the walker,
Walt Whitman's "lighthouse" on an "inland sea,"
crowded now but unsubmerged by towers,
and seen from building fronts that call up kings:
Renaissance columns, friezes, dormers, bellowing
gargoyles I've missed by never looking up.
I dogged him until his swaggering steps
merged with mine, and I ran into you —
a seething Hungarian immigrant, a Jew.

Hearing "the blab of the pave," I walked from the wharf's
wind-bent sloops and headed for Pfaff's
cave (now haunting a produce stand) to eat
with rowdies and squint at the theater crowd.
I waved at omnibus drivers — Pop Rice, Patsy Dee —
and elbowed by rings of stiff men in black coats
posing like unlighted streetlamps. How he
scowled at their boutonnières, and touched his beard,
no "washes and razors" for him, nor for you —
an out-of-fashion immigrant, a Jew.

These great houses breathe under their sites.
Gaslight shadows flicker on walls at night.
See the razed opera house on Astor Place
where Badiali sang, and Mario.
For Whitman at St. Ann's, high glorias
blended with deckhands' tunes on the Fulton ferry;
now, drifting under new talk on Broadway,

raw winds carry arias from *Lucia*
that Whitman heard, free-ticketed, and you,
gripping a spear, an immigrant Jew.

Whitman, in a synagogue on Crosby Street,
heard ancient vows in scenes "entirely new."
Men keened, their voices nameless deep-toned bells.
He wrote for the press: a "paneled wood" enclosure
held "sugar loaves" topped with glass and silver;
then, wrapped in white silk, the priest (he *thought*)
waved a parchment scroll. "The heart within
felt awed," he said, and his speech fell
under those minor chords that enchanted you
when you were there, an immigrant, a Jew

who read the Law and knew the ritual.
On Pike Street, where your father was a cantor,
you sang the sacred hymns to melodies
from oratorios you'd heard in concert halls,
and once, a sabbath chant, *Leha dodi,*
"Go, my beloved..." to a rollicking tune,
"There's One New York," struck up in a saloon.
Whitman woke to song; you crafted prayer,
whittling down the past to make it new
in your New York, an immigrant, a Jew.

In steamy rain, I zigzagged through your ghetto,
Orchard Street, Hester. Winter-melon bins
replace old pushcarts filled with knives and buttons;

on shop windows, brushstrokes read high to low,
not right-left, as your letters did, and now
graffiti on metal doors are calligraphic.
From here to City Hall you hiked, then on
to Washington Square's law school, looking back
on trees and weed-grown lots—all that you knew
of what was or would be, an immigrant Jew.

Move, move, move, to *con brio* scores
in your head. Praise all things fixed and loose.
Even when you can ride in horse-drawn cars,
walk, to feel unstuck cobbles through your soles,
to see leaves stuck to pebbled rectangles
like jewels in velvet bodices, to peer
from under elms at posters of Irving's *Lear*
and Olga Nethersole's *Camille*. In magic boots
dance on spangled streets that discover you
grateful to be an immigrant, a Jew.

Whitman you neither touched nor read, but here
men and women become one crowd and flow:
shoppers in sweats, kids with shrill radios,
temperance workers, livestock merchants, share
stagecoach clatter, trucks' din, vendors' whines,
and see towers rise: his, slate; yours, marble; mine,
Mondrian's skyscrapers made of the sky.
On misty days, I trek to the port and see
twin water-gazers, he, slouching, and you,
shifting about, a restless immigrant Jew

observing stone cut sharp, cut round: angular
capitals, curved shields; faces of gods.
I gather years carved into stone arcades
and cast on cornices, solid as ancestry,
while I hear a man drum jazz on a kitchen pail.
For Henry James, a walker in your day
you never knew, these streets hummed, bristled, lay
open to change: buildings were words that die
in air; he called them "impudently new"—
as you were then, a prospering immigrant Jew.

I find the Statue of Liberty draped in black
for President Garfield's assassination,
just as you did when your parents packed
in Hungary for free schools. Diamonds shine
in the boat's spume. A castle in the bay!
I've had to shape them, for your past was gone
under new asphalt. Now I hoard stone griffins
and cast-iron numbers, "1 8 7 3,"
on red brick, combing history for you,
Grandfather Dave, an immigrant, a Jew.

NEW NETHERLAND, 1654

Pardon us for uttering a handful
of words in *any* language, so cut loose
are we from homes, and from His name that is still
nameless, blessed be He. We raised a prayer house—

that is, we broke new wood for one, but some
tough burned it, snarling: "Carve only stones for the dead."
Damp ground, no fire, no psalm we all remember.
But tall ships anchor here, and at low tide,

people with wheat-colored hair look out to sea,
just as we'd searched for land. "Pray if you must,"
my father said, "and when prayer fails, a story,
if it is all you have, will do." Months past,

we left Recife's forced-worship laws in the year
of *their* Lord sixteen hundred and fifty-four, for our new
world, old-country Amsterdam. Leagues seaward,
Spanish pirates slaughtered our scant crew,

and all that was left of us (friends wheezed
their last while they ragged us on) rose up on deck
and tossed our bags in the sea. We watched the wake
turn silver: kiddish wine cups, hanging bowls,

a candelabrum for the promised altar,
carved pointers. Books' pages curled and sank,
prayer shawls ballooned and, soaking, spiraled downward.
Just as we stared, again we heard swords clank—

a French ship, the *Ste. Catherine* (her prow had shone
gold on a gray horizon), came to our
port side and rescued us. In that commotion
on deck, we crouched below—not out of fear,

I swear, but stunned by luminous words
that echoed oddly—beautifully—like lightning
flickering through palls of thickset clouds.
A jaunty captain rasped to us in hiding:

"Where are you bound?"

                       "Amsterdam. Old country."
"Where?"
        "Amsterdam."
              "Antilles?"
                     "No, Amsterdam."
"Yes, yes. Nieuw *Am*sterdam. I'll see
you get there safely." He meant well, bless him.

Ste. Catherine sailed to land at its tip no larger
than a meadow, fanned out at its sides:
Manhattan Island. Our new master,
Stuyvesant, lashed us with phrases, *wheffs, guzzads,*

that stung but were not fathomed, mercifully,
when we came on a Sabbath, more than twenty
men, women, a baby born at sea.
Still cursing, he let us land, and heard our praise,

then disappeared among lank citizens
with faded skin who stride to the bay and brood
on water that we trust and dread, and listen
to tales unstamped by laws and never sacred.

The Button Box

A sea animal stalked its prey
slithering under her bed, and gorged
on buttons torn from castaways;
ever unsated, it grew large

until it became a deity
spewing out buttons in a fire
of brass for blazers, delft or ruby
for shirts — and dangerous. You'd hear

it snarl when the beds were being made.
It ate stray pins and shot out poison.
But Mother, who stuffed its wooden frame,
scooped up waterfalls of suns,

enamel moons, clocks, cameos,
carved pinwheels, stars, tiny "Giottos,"
peacocks strutting out at sundown,
FDR's profile, flags of Britain,

silver helmets, all with missions.
Mother sewed ballerinas set
in circles on your satin dress,
onyx buttons that would join

you, collar to hood, at graduation;
she would find in the creature's lair
"bones" of an army officer,
"pearls" of a war bride's dressing gown;

nights when the radio hissed *dive bombers,*
Mother dreamed that she could right
the world again by making sure
you had your buttons, sewed on tight.

HOME MOVIE

Just then the squeaky camera caught
a sun crystal that haloed trees,
blurred fences, light dousing the light,
then twitched, and quivered into focus,

as I entered the child I was,
primped for the film in a ruffled smock,
touching the big hepaticas
I'd never seen in Central Park,

then pivoting to see my mother's
long arms arc through foamy water,
stroke by feathery stroke, and soar,
her white cap lost then found in glare,

and I, gasping in pride, in awe,
recalled a newsreel's dreadful flare
as warplanes fired at refugees,
mother and son, *people like us,*

then watched her rise up at the shore,
step to a tango, snap a towel,
and ran to her, eyes wide with all
I'd know of perfect form — and fear.

SITE:

The absence of a house. A negative image,
listed at wrong addresses in the guidebooks;
in fact, invisible. Still, it invites
what negative capability the heart

can muster—not simply to observe
the sun's glare on a jet's wing before sunrise,
but in dark rooms to hear a lost friend's laughter.
Take the house at 19 Washington Square,

the one with no brass plaque that claims
it's the site of a house in a book by Henry James.
When the late sun reddens the auburn bricks,
stare until stone steps turn to white marble,

Ionic columns flank the wooden door,
and frayed roses in the yard become
bold peonies restrained by iron fences
handwrought with lyres, Greek frets, acanthus leaves.

Peer through needlepoint lace above a balcony,
and find a woman at a writing table
in a red gown and shawl chosen so "they,
and not she, would look well," and know

that things survive in their sites, in the ghosts of houses,
linger in the incandescent images
of what we imagine has occurred: the parlor
after the guests have gone, the broken phrase

somebody whistled once; the theater's curtain
that holds the mark of the dancer's perilous leap
skyward—the flexed plié, the twist and spin
so high it seemed he would never descend.

CROSSING THE SQUARE

Squinting through eye-slits in our balaclavas,
we lurch across Washington Square Park
hunched against the wind, two hooded figures
caught in the monochrome, carrying sacks

of fruit, as we've done for years. The frosted, starch-
stiff sycamores make a lean Christmas tree
seem to bulk larger, tilted under the arch
and still lit in three colors. Once in January,

we found a feather here and stuffed the quill
in twigs to recall that jay. The musical fountain
is here, its water gone, a limestone circle
now. Though rap succeeds the bluegrass strains

we've played in it, new praise evokes old sounds.
White branches mimic visions of past storms;
some say they've heard ghosts moan above this ground,
once a potter's field. No two stones are the same,

of course: the drums, the tawny pears we hold,
are old masks for new things. Still, in a world
where fretted houses with façades are leveled
for condominiums, not much has altered

here. At least it's faithful to imagined
views. And, after all, we know the sycamore
will screen the sky in a receding wind.
Now, trekking home through grit that's mounting higher,

faces upturned to test the whirling snow,
in new masks, we whistle to make breath-clouds form
and disappear, and form again, and O,
my love, there's sun in the crook of your arm.

Notes from Underground: W. H. Auden on the Lexington Avenue IRT

Hunched in a corner seat, I'd watch him pass
riders who gaped at headlines: "300 DEAD,"
and, in their prized indifference to all
others, were unaware he was one who heard
meter in that clamor of wheels on rails.

Some days I took the local because he did:
He sank down into plastic, his bruised sandals
no longer straining with the weight of him;
there, with the frankness of the unacquainted,
I studied his face, a sycamore's bark

with lichen poking out of crevices.
His eyes lifted over my tattered copy
of his *Selected Poems,* then up to where
they drilled new windows in the car and found,
I guessed, tea roses and a healing fountain.

All memories are echoes: some whisper,
others roar, as this does. Dazed by war,
I, who winced at thunder, knew that train
screeched "DISASTER!" How it jolted and veered,
station after station, chanting *Kyrie*

eleison, while metal clanged on metal
and bulbs went dim. Peering at tracks, I heard,
"Still persuade us to rejoice." I glimpsed
a worn sandal, turned, and then my eyes
met his eyes that rayed my underworld.

GOD'S LETTERS

When God thought up the world,
the alphabet letters
whistled in his crown,
where they were engraved
with a pen of fire,
each wanting to begin
the story of Creation.

S said, I am Soul.
I can Shine out
from within your creatures.
God replied, I know that,
but you are Sin, too.

L said, I am Love,
and I brush away malice.
God rejoined, Yes,
but you are Lie,
and falsehood is not
what I had in mind.

P said, I am Praise,
and where there's a celebration,
I Perform
in my Purple coat.
Yes, roared God,
but at the same time,
you are Pessimism—
the other side of Praise.

And so forth.

All the letters
had two sides or more.
None was pure.
There was a clamor
in paradise, words,
syllables, shouting
to be seen and heard
for the glory
of the new heavens and earth.

God fell silent,
wondering,
How can song
rise from that commotion?

Rather than speculate,
God chose B,
who had intoned,
Bashfully, Boldly,
Blessed is *his* name.

And he made A
first in the Alphabet
for admitting, I am All —
a limitation
and a possibility.

Urban Bestiary

Throw back your head and see them
hunt you down Amsterdam
with pop eyes, knifeblade ears,
gaps weathered into scars,
mouths that cry and drain
waterfalls of rain.

Gargoyles. Bas-reliefs
worn smooth as buffalo nickels.
And carved beasts — no, not beasts
but pied horrors: animals,
men and women, torn,
then tacked together again.

Hear them shriek and howl.
One springs from a cornice,
another squats on a wall,
a third has wings, fishtail,
and hooves, all at once
to fly, swim, leap, and prance.

Cross streets, turn down alleys;
they'll spy you blocks away.
Sages with leafy beards,
kings with fangs, goat ears,
act out court murder scenes
bloodied by falling suns.

Hybrid monsters teach us
waking and dreams are one:
our fears, urges, and loves
sit high on towers of sandstone,
and poke up from the flat
bedrock of the heart.

EXPULSION

Half rotten, half sweet,
it lay on the ground for days
before I tried it,

and offered another
to my love, who said,
"I've never liked apples."

When I walked on,
he ate it, core and all.
And that's when it began.

We bought enough Rome Beauties
to make apple marmalade
and apple chutney—

then curries, soufflés,
pirozhki.
We grew restless,

even before the storm
cut off our water supply,
and winds lopped the elm

that cracked over telephone wire.
I remember
how in crisp air

the sun lit the sheep laurel
and fell, along with quiet.
He called the perennials

by names once unfamiliar to us,
each with a resonance:
monkshood, purple iris,

foxglove, nightshade;
some we tended,
others grew wild,

recurring gifts.
But all was not right.
There were shrill insects,

scorpions, snaky vines
that twisted up cedars
and strangled white pines.

Here in the city,
things are less clear;
a rickety

ambulance snorts,
carrying the half dead,
a pedestrian shot

during a robbery,
while toddlers embrace
twenty blocks away.

That square of street
not covered with grime
glitters in moonlight.

My love does not
give names to anything.
Instead, he falls silent

before a grove
of trees among buildings.
We cherish what little we have:

one side is bright,
the other dark.
We praise it.

FALSE MOVE

Hearing a thud, as though a ball had struck
my windowpane, seeing a feathery mass
cling to the spot, I peered outside, fearfully
braced for some creature, writhing or inert.

It was a grackle, changing glass to air.
Dead still, the bird was on his feet. Too dazed
to fear my hand, he tilted a stiff head,
opened a knifelike beak but made no sound,

hunched an iridescent back. He's done for:
that polished purple, ebony, and brown
will sink. With glassy eyes, he saw a clearing
larger than his cage of air allowed,

tested its limits, darted as though worlds
could bend. My ground is cumbrous earth that sun
can fire, storms erode. Those silver hills
beyond the hemlocks actually are mountains:

I've scaled their ledges, narrowly escaping
grooves. One step too far, one double image
can kill, I knew, and faltered. Then the bird
lowered his nape, compressed his body, flew.

The Wedding

Late spring in Caesaria, Herod's harbor,
now a city of Roman ruins, quiet
but for gull cries in the white-hot light
of midday. People gather at the shore

as if to see a sword dance, to hear drums
and dagger-beats on shields — the pre-biblical
rites of this region — not the nuptials
of military lovers: agile, slim

army border-guards on active duty
wearing pearl-white wedding costumes, she,
satin and lace, he, linen, stiffly
pressed. Seeming too young to fight or marry,

they pose for photographs, the sea exploding
on rocks, and, shoes cast off, run on hot sand
to the marriage canopy, a covering
to cast off demons. It snaps in high wind,

their sacred roof, a dazzling cotton
embroidered prayer shawl whose supporting poles
are rifles held by three men and a woman
in combat fatigues. There, before them all,

a rabbi intones the seven benedictions,
offers wine, hears vows and blesses them,
and blesses children who sing psalms. At sundown,
when the bridal pair change into uniforms,

a shot rings out. A woman screams and falls.
Three of the groom's attendants grab the rifles
that held the canopy, fall to the ground
at the stammer of guns, rub faces with wet sand,

and, shouldering their weapons, run to the sea,
firing at men who creep out of a dinghy
that's dragged aground. One of the intruders,
his buoyant gait so like the bride's

that he seems an invited cousin, drops to the shore,
face down. Another stranger staggers
a few yards, bleeding, his stubby fingers
frozen on his gun. Bodies pitch forward,

arms and legs flail. Silence. White garments strewn
like a book's blown pages, the groom bends down
to lift the prayer shawl that lies, torn,
mud-splattered. He folds it, kisses it, then

flings his red beret to the darkening
sand. Leading his bride to a small car,
he turns back for a time, as though to hear,
through mounting wave sounds, what the children sang.

Julian of Norwich

Warped in the window-diamonds of my cell,
distorted, outsize primroses unfold:
I see all manner of things that shall be well.

Eyeless men with plague-sores come to chapel,
hungry, with blood-soaked poultices, and cold.
Warped in the window-diamonds of my cell,

they lurch and fall, inert. Another dead bell.
Their king gone, my King blesses (dressed in gold,
I see) all manner of things that shall be well.

Hermits recoil. If I were to foretell
doom, monks would believe. Instead, I'm called
warped. In the window-diamonds of my cell

are men who know Black Death and wars, and tell
of starless night, and will until I'm old,
I see. All manner of things that shall be well

deceive: dense glass in quarrel panes can spell
disaster, lunacy. Faces are bold,
warped in the window-diamonds of my cell.
I see all manner of things that shall be well.

RESCUE IN PESCALLO

Neither do I believe in miracles,
although at times an actual homely image
can lift the eyes and the expectations. Pale,
dark-haired, severe, a woman from the village

of Pescallo said a statue of Christ
had washed up on these shores and startled schoolboys,
who called some local men, fishing for trout.
They listened closely, as for a drowned man's cries

of life, and stared at the figure, carved in oak,
the body painted white, the hair and beard
black. They hauled it up and carried it
to the Church of San Giacomo, a good

kilometer away, where she'd last seen it, lying
under a fresco of the Deposition
ascribed to Perugino. "Now the painting
may well be a replica, but that wooden

figure is unique, for what it is,"
she said, and frowned. "You know the yellow-white
scant flower, the anemone? It grows
among these stones, in shade. So too that

carving bobbed on the waves and steered through ice.
I guess it came as flotsam, possibly
junked, along with boards that had been pews,
cast out of a ruined chapel in a nearby

harbor on the lake." Rapt, she continued,
"Or perhaps, in transit, it fell overboard,
not to be retrieved until, by God,
it loomed up here." The woman halted, stirred

by some dark memory, and threw a tarpaulin
over her stone sarcophagus. A sculptor
who modeled snaky forms, her studio once
a stable on a villa near the water,

she led me down an aisle of cypresses
that trapped a cloud, and would, until the wind
rose. It seemed we glided in a tapestry
of towers and doves, all things enlarged beyond

normal scale in the clear air. I gathered
the statue baffled her. She dismissed events
that wanted proof, and knew the dense-grained wood,
the size and weight, the tides, the precise moment

it surfaced, but she inferred that it had come
—like penstrokes in her drawings for sarcophagi—
from a chillier place than she could fathom,
try as she did. Returning to the story,

she said, "That day, the south wind we call *breva*
brought ghostly mist that dimmed the bald horizon,
welding sky and water into metal.
In fog, the people saw the mud-smirched, lean

Christ walk through their spiraling thin streets,
hoisted on the shoulders of two fishermen,
staggering, really, head, nailed feet, and torso
one seesaw plank that passed the shops, the one

waterfront caffè, and the pier. It sidled
onto the Via Garibaldi, where
it nearly grazed a bench when one man buckled
and fell. Seeing the statue waver

and lean a bit, clerks left their shops, doors open,
to set it right. Determined carabinieri,
who'd seen the pallid relic pass their station
in mist, stopped traffic. Blank-faced passersby

joined a kind of ritual parade that went
to the church door, where nuns and merchants set
the mottled body, scrubbed, dabbed with new paint,
on a slab inside the crypt." The woman thought

none of the villagers knew what had happened,
in their minds' eyes, or were the better for it.
"They're all retarded cousins in Pescallo,"
she muttered to her watch, an hour late.

She had shunned Daylight Time, since, as a girl,
she heard Il Duce rule it into law;
she doubted love, distrusted friendship, grateful
simply to look, bear witness, and withdraw.

Charcoal-haired, with eyes both fixed and empty,
and moon-blanched skin, she carved heads in the style
of Donatello, then, in Milan, she woke
to obscure archbishops' tombs in purple

marble, amazed at life flesh-eaters gave,
and made sarcophagus relief. Tenaciously,
she chiseled Hindu deities, brave
princes and governors in vaults. Not airy

avatars but weighty men and women
danced on her coffins. Curiously, they changed,
each more itself when its contours were gone
to others in the clusters she arranged.

Finishing one sculpture, then another,
she ticked off years, then bent under great losses.
Lifeless as crystal, she intoned that after
her son had died of leukemia in Venice,

her husband gone, she felt her own life flicker.
Somehow her forms assumed finer detail,
although she noticed actual things grow weaker,
their outlines vague. Searching for new soil,

she wandered to this country, where she saw,
in early spring, a branch of apricot
in bloom among stiff twigs. A week of sun
had undone heavy frost, and startled it.

Seeing the terraced valley, where small houses
were terra-cotta rectangles that shone
through haze, near ancient olive trees and fortresses,
she set about to cut resistant limestone

and red marble to life in the sarcophagi,
visions of tombs for her imagined kings;
she cut them into birth as unexpectedly
as violets spring from rock. "People and things

existed for me here in fabulous harmony,
so natural it seemed strange. Although the white
citrus trees and pines covered the land,
chapels and piers were never out of sight."

She smoothed a canvas skirt, her mica eyes
fastened on snow-covered mountain peaks. The task
of creating angular deities in friezes
was good. But still, occasionally, at dusk,

she said, she watched the steamboat from Varenna
furrow the lake, and hurried to the landing
to meet the boy whose death she'd dulled away
in those gray moments. She shuddered, recalling

sunsets obscured by vapor. "Only the chirr
of motors told me where I was. Mist fell,
and dimmed out the eroded planks, the pier's
geometry, lake scum, the rotted guardrail.

"Fog beckoned me. And also, as the south wind
moves, I brought an inner mist that blurred
or made my universe, although the mind
saved clearness for the work. One day I heard

San Giacomo's bells before I reached the wharf.
Purchasing wine and olives in a store,
I faltered; then, for all I scorned belief
(it was at vespers), I tugged at the door."

Cautious as a night marauder, stranger
to her first house, she stepped gingerly
behind bowed shoulders, found a bench, and glanced
at the bone-white relic washed ashore and quietly

repaired, the soggy belly bleached, the pupils
glossed. Perhaps a craftsman from Bellano
modeled the piece some eighty years before,
and, after he finished, saw wood glow.

Her neighbors had renewed the harrowed image
that survived somehow. "Yes, a miracle,"
she said aloud, and halted at the one
word that meant too much, explained too little.

Watching a carpenter from Bergamo
turn to regard the idol he had planed,
she saw at last her own figures as metaphors,
more alive than men, more dead than stone.

There, as the north wind rose up in the mountains,
she knew the statue held fast just as limestone
and marble tombs are genuine. But then,
unlike those sculptures, her mortal son

was of a transient brightness, and could never
return or be restored. Without repeating
those random thoughts, she never searched the pier
again for the dead child. Her story ending,

I knew volcanic tremors had ripped open
her eyes when that zinc-white log floated up here.
Her voice was fathoms down when she asserted,
"Christ rose on these shores, eleven years

ago, and on this day, the eve of Tenebrae
—the holy litany of gathering shadows—
this last week of Lent, before Good Friday
and the Great Vigil." Nodding at a yellow

primrose, she measured days as kilos verify
an infant's being, then said she saw light flare
through clouds long after dusk. She turned to me,
knowing I understood her words, and, more,

the truth of radiant images that rise,
unbidden, from the bottom of the mind's
dark waters, to survive whirlpools and surface,
mud-soaked, tattered, worn, to beach on sand,

bodiless, lake-drenched carriers of keenest
vision, loosened, when given legs and heads,
to clarify the mist, just as she freed
souls of those whose bodies she had made.

El Greco's *Saint James, the Less*

This moonlight fractured into mere threads of stars
shines now on eyes indifferent or turned to some
    white peak inside that none but he sees,
   he, and those taught by the painter's vision.

Light falls on blue-and-red robes whose shadows are
black mouths that cry of glare that has deepened them.
    One hand unfurls; its lambent fingers
   curve down, then curl up, a torch upended.

That hand recalls a starburst that hung from a
white pine; it turned in altering light, and its
    green needles fell away and pointed at
   random, a fan on its branch, an uncertain omen.

One day a mourning dove that was stammering
faint notes flew low, splayed out like the tangle of
    white pine. The bird, the tree, and now that
   hand of Saint James are one form. The dove gone,

light stays, its glow the mind's brightness, gleam of a
first day on earth in tales of Creation when
    one beam that God devised, before the
   sun, would have shown us the world in one glance.

CARRION

The chipmunk's carcass lay flat on a stone
stair that led to rooms above the shed.
Hind legs, a tail, a strand of wine-red beads
and innards, showed whose body it had been.

One step above the corpse, a cat discreetly
unfurled, with eyes half closed, guarding the kill.
Caretakers had fed him well, and still
the animal had craved some swifter prey.

The cat himself, ill-used, had been abandoned.
Boarded at stables here to calm the horses,
he was released after the racing season
passed, and found a temporary place

on this estate. Later, he would be free
to forage in the woods. The horse he eased
"will make a good brood mare when her racing days
are done," the auctioneer said. Rings of grief:

Scissors, paper, rock, I sang as a child.
Scissors cut paper that covers rock
that pulverizes scissors. Still I'm locked
in that small circle, flaying, being flayed.

Small fingers whipped my wrist: bland-mannered Catherine
was paper. I, being rock, would lash
my dearest Ann, with flimsy yellow hair,
for being scissors. So the wheel turned, and turns.

I touched the chipmunk's glittering cadaver,
then buried it. The cat quivered to stand,
warning my hand that stole the prize he murdered.
Beyond the steps, a spruce raised votive candles.

Walking through double rows of junipers
that day, I glanced away from cruelty,
or so I tried: a hawk warped in midair
called back the day I watched a herring gull

circle to land, scoop up a turtle, glide
upward again, and drop it to crack its shell.
My neighbor shot the gardener who denied
he ever cared, and who was seen at Bill's

drinking bourbon with a new lover.
"She seemed too old, too stoical, for murder.
She won't get off," a villager asserted —
sadly, I thought. I never knew the killer,

had seen her only, taut as a dry leaf
someone had kicked on the ground, chilly, slight,
her skin worn porcelain, her long body
angular in stride, flexed, as in flight.

That night my feet, my elongated thighs,
stiffened and went cold; then, as I lay
counting the stars, my carrion entrails
flickered below my eaten chest, my eyes.

Two Trees

For DAVID AND RHONDA

Ancient borassus palms, masculine and feminine,
rise on this coast as they soared in Eden,

and yearn to join yet stand, earth, sky between them.
See them now, after the storm —

call it a whirlwind, or someone's cross phrase —
cracked the mangos' trunks but spared these trees.

Each closes leafy fans above hard wood
that wraps the visionary self inside.

In a Van Eyck painting, man and wife are seen
and see: a convex mirror throws back curtains,

well-wishers, outside the viewer's province;
and in a Beckett play, a man listens

to himself on a reel-to-reel recorder
speak of a brighter but unwanted summer.

So the self gathers, multiplies, alone.
In this replanted Eden, newly grown

palms breathe free, unbent by other palms,
and bear fruit when they are ready, in their time.

THE LUXEMBOURG GARDENS

1. GUSTAVE FLAUBERT

The statue suits him: a sad oracle's
head rests on a pedestal that rises
from the shoulders of a bench, as if an angel
had scooped it up from the mud and flown it higher

than the park's fence. Viewing a wide allée
of horse chestnut trees that, even now, pour
rain in sudden brightness, sly Flaubert
perches like an osprey above his prey.

No pigeon lights on his shadowy head
in blackening stone. As in Rouen, he tries
"to live in an ivory tower," but, indeed,
he finds "a tide of shit beats at its walls,"

an ebb-and-flow he scrutinized, as now.
Unlike his friend George Sand, who reclines
on sunlit grass some yards away, and glows
in white stone, closed book pressed to waistline,

he is made not to be seen, but to see:
facing him are chairs of green iron
on which, minutes ago, a man and a woman
had sat and glared, perhaps angrily.

"Speech is like a rolling machine that stretches
the feelings it expresses," Flaubert says,
then lets his eyes go vacant like the eyes
of a café-sitter who stares at passersby

and focuses when a friend appears.
To see it all is to know the deepest layer,
and yet he must see everything. He lingers
now on a woman combing yellow hair,

and notices her chapped hands, baggy jeans,
then gazes at the walk. Screened by trees,
a mime in whiteface practices slow turns;
a man in gold-lace sandals ambles by;

a greyhound sniffs at an empty chair.
A *gardien* with a high hat scolds a vagrant
sprawled on the grass, then smiles at a *garde d'enfant*
wheeling a stroller, the arms of her sweater

knotted at her throat. The officer
looks up at the statue—jaw-length hair,
the mustache cut like a bow's streamers—
and strides away, as if he did not hear:

"Idols must not be touched; the gold paint
rubs off on our fingers." Stone ears take in
the crunch of polished patent leather
boots on the dirt path, the *clack clack clack*

of high-heeled shoes on a cobbled walk nearby.
I hide the leaf I stole to identify,
and know I am *his* subject, not he mine.
I marvel at his keen glance. He replies:

"Nobody loves praise more than I, and praise
bores me." Searching for someone who would "practice
virtue without believing in it," he sees,
and his sight is love; he never loses

his critical remove, as does his Emma,
not even for a scarf that crooks like a huge gold comma
or the arc of a red ball that shines in flight,
catching the strong but tentative morning light.

2. THE GOOD WOMEN

Who caught them this way? Shapely stone
queens and other *grandes dames* lurk in trees,
cousins to the Statue of Liberty,
another classy vamp. They are made of contradiction:

Geneviève, a saint whose prayers saved Paris
from the invader, clenches her long fingers,
and peers through leaves,
                                    round bosom, snaky braids;

Queen Matilda, duchess of Normandy,
of the sword and crown, the cross and the fleur-de-lis,
rests the tall sword
                              against a narrow waist.

Waving a scepter, Queen Blanche of Castille,
who rescued the kingdom from rebels,
frees one hand
                          to clutch a billowing skirt,

while Charlemagne's mother, Bertha of the Great
Feet, holds her king, Pepin the Short,
and his throne
                          in her unsceptered hand

near fierce Queen Margaret of Anjou,
"she-wolf of France, and worse than wolves of France,"
who glides,
                      clasping her son to a curvy bodice,

and there is Hugo de Sade's wife, Laura de Noves,
possibly Petrarch's bold (here reticent) love,
beside Clémence Isaure,

                    who leans on one hip.

Under a wide-eyed Louise de Savoy,
who, not so simply, joined another queen
to arrange a peace treaty of Cambrai.
I slide into an iron chair, and frown

at an unseemly décolletage
some Beaux Arts sculptor dreamed had been the rage,
wrong, or at the least, chilly for court.
Then, as I leave, I watch a girl recite:

"M-A-R-G-U-E-R-I-T-E D-E F-R-A-N-C-E," Margaret
of Angoulême, queen of Navarre, who wrote
tales that inspired Rabelais, and here —
           (one hand touches the cheek, the other holds flowers)

coquette — allays my doubts: all oxymorons,
saints, muses, consorts, sages, scholars,
mothers of, daughters of, sirens, leaders,
flame up in paradox — those are the queens.

From

THE PAINTINGS OF OUR LIVES

(2001)

PRAYER

For AGHA SHAHID ALI

Yom Kippur: wearing a bride's dress bought in Jerusalem,
I peer through swamp reeds, my thought in Jerusalem.

Velvet on grass. Odd, but I learned young to keep this day
just as I can, if not as I ought, in Jerusalem.

Like sleep or love, prayer may surprise the woman
who laughs by a stream, or the child distraught in Jerusalem.

My Arab dress has blue-green-yellow threads
the shades of mosaics hand-wrought in Jerusalem

that both peoples prize, like the blue-yellow Dome of the Rock,
like strung beads-and-cloves, said to ward off the drought in
        Jerusalem.

Both savor things that grow wild—coreopsis in April,
the rose that buds late, like an afterthought, in Jerusalem.

While car bombs flared, an Arab poet translated
Hebrew verses whose flame caught in Jerusalem.

And you, Shahid, sail Judah Halevi's sea as I,
on Ghalib's, course like an Argonaut in Jerusalem.

Stone lions pace the sultan's gate while almonds bloom
into images, Hebrew and Arabic, wrought in Jerusalem.

No words, no metaphors, for knives that gore flesh
on streets where the people have fought in Jerusalem.

As this spider weaves a web in silence,
may Hebrew and Arabic be woven taut in Jerusalem.

Here at the bay, I see my face in the shallows
and plumb for the true self our Abraham sought in Jerusalem.

Open the gates to rainbow-colored words
of outlanders, their sounds untaught in Jerusalem.

My name is Grace, Chana in Hebrew—and in Arabic.
May its meaning, "God's love," at last be taught in Jerusalem.

GOD SPEAKS

Before the hour I cried, "Let there be light!"
I tossed out some three hundred early versions.
Revisions help. What clatter in the firmament,
though, when mountains fell, stars fizzled out.

This work is my best, at least for now.
I called. I named each thing, and "it was so."
I cannot tell you how, from heaven to seas
to people, all sprang up wanting to be.

The methods I advise are more precise —
Noah's ark, for instance, gopher wood,
three stories high, side entrance, and a window.
Here when I said "the waters," oceans rose.

Worlds are never finished, only abandoned.
Yet this one came alive when there were woods
for creeping things, dry land for men and women,
the evening and the morning. *They* were good.

Creation had been done before, of course —
in legend. Same formless waste and darkness,
but with one change: the Babylonians
have many gods. Always I work alone.

Eve's Unnaming

Not horses, but roan
against the blue-green bay,

not crocuses, but wings
folded over suns,

not rhododendrons, but fire that wilts
to straw in the rain.

How to tag
stone, shell, gull,

hands enfolding lamb's-ear,
a bee sucking the delphinium,

when the sea writes and revises,
breaks, pours out, recoils,

when the elm's leaves
turn silver at dawn.

To see in the dark
the south window strew flowers

on the chapel floor,
or wind peel a sand rose,

is unnamable,
like joy,

like my love's grin
between a cap and a jacket.

Names are for things
we cannot own.

Chaim Soutine

Hunger was bearable, but not their voices
resonant as clock chimes in his head:
Thou shalt not make unto thee any graven image.

Gaunt, bleary-eyed, he filched coins from a shelf,
not for food, but for red and yellow pencils
to draw a madman who had God's fixed stare.

Locked in a cellar, grasping at cracks of light,
unrepentant, he heard his parents wail,
or any likeness of anything in heaven above;

He sketched the rabbi, trying to uncover
red-yellow rays beneath the prayer shawl.
Thrashed, he left his village of Smilovitch

and painted. Years passed. Over and again
he'd make a still life of a dead goose, hen —
or that is in the earth beneath —

this one a hanging turkey, beak agape,
wings splayed as though still flying. Days and nights
he jabbed red-yellow strokes on canvas

to make the wingspread, damning, pitying
wings that reach for light and, falling, rise —
or that is in the water under the earth —

burned wings of Icarus; his father's hands,
gnarled fingers mending coats, the hands of Christ.
Where God had been, the turkey shone, flesh-colored

as naked man, over "Soutine," in blood,
and he sang to drown their sobbing, now grown louder:
Thou shalt not make unto thee any graven image.

Poem Ending with a Phrase from the Psalms

Here where loss spins the hickory's dry leaves,
rolls miles under wheels, and bleaches reeds
that shone wine-red, I invoke a rose
still rising like a choir, past its prime
on a spindly bush that bore scarce blooms,
as I wake to hear a jay screech like a gate
swung open, and see your hand enfolding mine
on linen: *teach us to number our days.*

Psalm for an Anniversary

Praise to boredom: to the summer solstice,
to our long marriage, its minutes dissolving
into hours here on the roof at sunset
as we watch shadows print their towers on buildings

while impersonal windows blink and darken.
Praise to recurrences: worn benches, laughter,
white roses you brought home, old army talk
I want to hear again. Bless the ruptures

healed, faint as wire dolls in the park below us —
the skiff I boarded once that coursed the bay,
leaving your island; that was urgency,
not this, when voices fall, eased by the sky's

arc over a bridge. In lulls, the mind
can see another city above this one,
ironic, hybrid as a string of puns.
Cupolas and the pyramids cut the skyline;

a red-brick campanile shelters a water tank;
and nuns in their high habits sail in pairs
to a ruined chapel over a warehouse,
its empty sockets glaring salmon pink.

A frieze of horses has survived — that is,
in replica — as though it were eternal,
while we, flawed with mistakes, who thought the skins
we shed would be our last, survey a steeple,

a tower clock, a dome. Praise to the sun
that flares and flares again in fierce explosions
even after sunset, to muddy rivers
that glow vermilion now, to second chances.

BALM IN GILEAD

"Is there no balm in Gilead?" So cries
dour Jeremiah in granite tones.
"There is a balm in Gilead," replies
a Negro spiritual. The baritone

who chants it, leaning forward on the platform,
looks up, not knowing his voice is a rainstorm
that rinses air to reveal earth's surprises.
Today, the summer gone, four monarch butterflies,

their breed's survivors, sucked a flower's last blooms,
opened their wings, orange-and-black stained glass,
and printed on the sky in zigzag lines,
watch bright things rise: winter moons, the white undersides
of a California condor, once thought doomed,
now flapping wide like the first bird from ashes.

No Strings

Marble seated harp player,
        Cycladic, early third millennium B.C.

At times your silences call back a harpist
that glows, pale yellow marble in late sun,
carved in the Cyclades, maker unknown,

seated, the head thrown back, arms gliding free,
hands curved to pluck a harp shaped like an alpha,
stringless, frame joined to shoulder, branch to tree.

The time: nearly five thousand years ago.
One hour ago. As when we met, a lifetime,
a minute past. We gazed at it, at him,

that day and the bare harp rang, drowning out
the museum's clamor and a traffic siren.
How song flows out of awe that grows in silence,

and how all things begin, alpha, with song.
At last you said the statue came along
when someone, name obscure, offered a prayer,

plied emery, and buffed a man on a chair
who'd raise a stringless harp and play the air.
Nodding, I thought of seeing in the wings

of a hushed hall a flutist who looked up
while fingering imaginary stops,
then strode onstage and made cadenzas soar.

In the Café

Blue notes like words cry out to one another.
Harsh trumpet phrases, open-horn — like rage
dug into earth, then risen to huge tones —

vault the night air and, muted, fall.
At bedtime, Father read a poem in Polish,
lines memorized and chanted. There were trumpets

and bells in his voice that held back the night
with wizard-talk I never understood,
words that told secrets, padlocks to pry open,

spells against the dark. My father learned them
from his brother, Jan, who cursed hunger in song,
and who was found at last on a dirt road

beaten, frozen, dead. Father fled Poland
and seldom spoke of Jan, but still I heard,
under his satin tones, Jan's mockery,

blue trumpet notes that sang to one another,
secrets that unfurled like silver waves
far out at sea. Then traveled closer, closer.

Carnegie Hill Birdlore

Today a robin hopped between stalled cars,
picked bright excelsior from a truck's cargo,
flew it to a ledge, then dived for more.
Odd bird: with Central Park's gardens so near,

why not beak catmint or hydrangea twigs?
Our idols vary. The white unicorn
that shines, hunted and slain, in tapestries,
assured the queen who prized it of the regal

death, hers of the heart. Now, inside towers
sequined with lights are more lights, gleaming icons:
a gilded wooden saint, an ebony Shiva,
halogen-dappled vine leaves. Stones

lodged under a garden lantern tell us,
weary, on dim streets, how we may wake
infused with light, like bits of agate glass
that beam with opals in an altar mosaic.

Downtown, in my brick aerie, the late sun
stripes a bare wall saffron, orange, and brown;
Bach on CDs, my love and I look down
from small but lustrous rooms, our residence.

BLUE DAWN

I see Viola float in on a plank
from the wreck, touch land, pocket a seashell
for luck, and, shivering, glide into a kingdom,

as once Long Island's settlers trudged ashore
and, though weary, took in blue-green forests
at sunrise, before lines furrowed the oak trees.

When his ship steamed into New York Harbor,
my father stood on deck in cramped, thin shoes
and watched blue rocks grow to be Ellis Island.

Sailing through fog at daybreak, his eyes burning
with the statue's unlit torch, how could he know
that one day he would walk on asphalt pavement

wearing a tweed coat, though still in cramped shoes.
Scant time for shops, he said, but I knew he chose
to save the blue wonder of what might be,

as I do now: slate flagstones going blue
in the not-yet-risen sun, an unopened iris,
the miracle of a yet unprinted page.

DECEMBER

Not the month for an angel. No gull soars,
no hawk swoops down from a TV antenna,
and a stone General Washington looks frail.
Teakettle steam rises as the sun falls,
no later than four. Darkness. Yet December
carries a hidden bass, like my shy neighbor

who cries out suddenly, "Lord, come by here."
Just as a pale sky glows blood red at sunset
on a blank day you can be seized—and blessed.
A window with drawn blinds like a sleeper's eye

throws back a glassy archangel that blazes
high, warped as if seen through water—not Michael,
but the Life Insurance Company's golden
pyramid that strews gold dust on black hair.

American Solitude

"The cure for loneliness is solitude."
—Marianne Moore

Hopper never painted this, but here
on a snaky path his vision lingers:

three white tombs, robots with glassed-in faces
and meters for eyes, grim mouths, flat noses,

lean forward on a platform, like strangers
with identical frowns scanning a blur,

far off, that might be their train.
Gas tanks broken for decades face Parson's

smithy, planked shut now. Both relics must stay.
The pumps have roots in gas pools, and the smithy

stores memories of hammers forging scythes
to cut spartina grass for dry salt hay.

The tanks have the remove of local clammers
who sink buckets and stand, never in pairs,

but one and one and one, blank-eyed, alone,
more serene than lonely. Today a woman

rakes in the shallows, then bends to receive
last rays in shimmering water, her long shadow

knifing the bay. She slides into her truck
to watch the sky flame over sand flats, a hawk's

wind arabesque, an island risen, brown
Atlantis, at low tide; she probes the shoreline

and beyond grassy dunes for where the land
might slope off into night. Hers is no common

emptiness, but a vaster silence filled
with terns' cries, an abundant solitude.

Nearby, the three dry gas pumps, worn
survivors of clam-digging generations,

are luminous, and have an exile's grandeur
that says: In perfect solitude, there's fire.

One day I approached the vessels
and wanted to drive on, the road ablaze

with dogwood in full bloom, but the contraptions
outdazzled the road's white, even outshone

a bleached shirt flapping alone
on a laundry line, arms pointed down.

High noon. Three urns, ironic in their outcast
dignity—as though, like some pine chests,

they might be prized in disuse — cast rays,
spun leaf-covered numbers, clanked, then wheezed

and stopped again. Shadows cut the road
before I drove off into the dark woods.

Storm Watch

Either it will kill me or I'll paint it,
Turner cried. The man who wore a top hat
and black coat to his easel had three sailors
lash him to the *Ariel*'s mast in shallows

of Harwich harbor. Four hours wiped out
by freezing wind. The earth lurched sideways
and the water's black, the sky's white
—his palette—churned up unremembered seas.

And I believe it. Outside my window,
snow drifts over the square's arch, wraps green benches,
and feathers trees. A man in a parka quits his car
in the empty street and stands unbent

to watch flakes blur the hours. When I look westward
into whiteness, as he does, toward the river,
years merge: I see that bruised sled new, and steer
down a hill (it was a mountain), my black terrier

kicking up diamonds. Suddenly I'm caught
in tarred ropes on a steamboat flashing signals
as new gusts cut ice into shards, waves
into arcs. I know that danger, that beauty

now—and it persists. In Turner's vision,
white clouds that seem calm, one after another,
riot in mobs. There's no end to that weather.
Even the cracks in oil are new explosions.

YOUNG WOMAN DRAWING, 1801

*Attribution changed from Jacques Louis David
to Constance Charpentier, and, most recently,
to Marie-Denise Villers, 1774–1821*

Subject and maker shed their names, and here
the Met displays that multinominal picture
on a brochure: self-portrait of the artist,
perhaps, ageless. She is not setting out,

pale in an empire dress, nor packing shawls
in a carriage trunk. As she sits forward, still,
she hopes only to gaze into a mirror
in shadow, sunlight falling on blank paper,

until her penstrokes dance, and ever after,
to slough off names and be one-who-has-seen-
glass-shine. How did it bloom in her, this hidden
boldness? Peering out from under wisps of amber

hair strayed from a chignon, taking pencil
to outsize sketchpad, she keeps a dark vigil,
while behind her, outside a shattered pane,
proud lovers laugh on a terrace in bright sun.

BLACK AND WHITE

BLACK: From *bhel*, "To shine, flash, burn; shining white."

White stones, frost, doves, icelight, icewind.
Wanting words for more white and more black,
Celan found the cliff where eyebright grew

in reams — Augentrost, Indian pipe —
his flower with white petals that dry black.
He gave them to his love, and ever after,

black boots, black whips, and black guns dried white.
Black-and-white shone out in terror then:
news headlines and a voiceless telephone,

the silhouette of a border guard. In peace
they brawl, hushed, fire in those icy tones.
My dreams are silent films in black-and-white,

a mime in whiteface dances his grief,
words cut the page, light glows inside the oak.
Now in our lives' solstice, we watch white

rise out of blackness. Sea spray. Under stars,
plankton in waves that roll in white-on-black;
at noon, the white-hot road comes clear of shadows.

Here, tulips blaze in light that has pried open
the cask of winter; trees lift bridal veils
and toss out blossoms that drift like snow.

A young man scatters blooms on his love's black shoulders.
A crow flickers white in a high elm,
mocking the raucous clash of black-and-white.

Margaret Fuller

The sea churns up a ghost of the *Elizabeth,*
sunk here in 1850, with the woman
who thought herself half man when she learned Latin
early in Cambridge, who honed a keen wit

"to keep the heart from breaking." All in all,
land sighted, others rescued, lulls in the gale,
I'd say she could have swum to shore. She had
that way with danger. In Scotland once,

trapped on a ledge, she danced cold mist away.
In Rome, she nursed the wounded, wrote of war,
but could not press her thoughts into one form
"for all the tides of life that flow within me."

How to return, when long ago she knew
everyone worth knowing here, when she
who shot the rapids stuck in Boston's craw.
And how to tell them of her love, Ossoli,

and of their new republic, lost—the rebels
dead, Rome gone. Twelve hours she had that morning
to swim homeward after the brig struck shoal.
Perhaps she stalled on the foredeck, avoiding

a half-welcoming shore; perhaps she spun
through waves, then turned, as a bird veers in flight
to glimpse its mate, and saw her lover caught
with their son, half native, half Italian,

watched breakers wrench the mainmast from the hull,
cried out once, twice, into the lashing wind,
then lost her torn self to the sea's wholeness.
Once in a storm, I found washed up on sand

a jetty's pole, and saw in it my own
splintered life's course. Before that gale,
I had swum partway out to her, and sea-miles
rolled out like the decades since she drowned.

Now I stand fast. Fire Island's opal
bay at high tide sucks amber rocks shot through
with quartz-glass silica, once El Dorado
to settlers half Old World and half New.

Far off, the lighthouse shines occulting beams
on sunken draggers. Only the sea is whole.
A split log or a chipped but vacant shell
the hermit crab crawls under is my home.

THE DANCERS

Turning to leave, she stands before a mirror
that picks up lights in sherry-colored hair.
A black/white picture's tucked inside the frame:
she and my father stand before that same

silvery mirror hung in her parents' house
in Brooklyn. He wears a tuxedo. She's
tossed a kimono over a satin dress,
hair brushed back and cropped like Sylvia Sidney's.

They're caught winging the air, kicking a high
rag as on a tightrope, showing off glossy
smiles to Uncle Josh, who tilts the camera—
before he spins and winds up the Victrola

to play "Blue Skies." Song ended, they will gather
swimsuits for after-revels near the shore,
and a beaded purse, then step off into stars.
It's the Depression. Dad is an actor

out of work. No money, no despair.
How could they know that I'd be born to shouts
of war; his family lost. Why do I fear
now for those bright kids dancing on the night

they went to a party in the sputtering Ford,
the job with rumble seat and running boards,
the mirror behind them catching the glimmer
of my father's top hat, my mother's hair.

BROOKLYN BRIDGE

From the beginning, it was life or death,
the maker and his son lost to the river
their bridge would hold down — one struck by a ferry,

the other by caisson bends — young Roebling's wife
learning math to redeem the family prophecy:
"It will be beautiful." And so it was, and is,

corseted to brace not merely horsecars
but trucks. Now, the sky vast after dense buildings,
I wander under Gothic towers and watch

trapezoids spring skyward, spun wire ropes
quivering in sunlight. All around me
today, like dancers stepping with unknown partners,

men and women travel east to Brooklyn,
set-jawed, some with kids in strollers,
then meet and sidle past those striding west.

"Cyclists dismount!" an unseen caller shouts,
and bikers obey. The crowd breaks for a woman
who lugs a canvas. Buckling some, she tacks

into the wind, not letting go. A man
carries roses, blooms pointed down. Some wild hope
in their striding cries "It will be beautiful,"

and raises ghosts: where walkway meets the road,
a vision of my grandmother in 1920,
belled skirt, braided red hair. She slithers under

her stalled Ford and out again, tarred black,
then cranks the engine. The cargo, prints
she's engraved on woodblocks with penlike

gouges kept on shelves, riling my grandfather
until he uttered "Flora!" twice, and cursed
the inky floors, then tromped out, slammed the door.

At twelve she'd walked the bridge to mark shirt collars
in a factory. Married young, she longed
to make black collars; she saw waves and sea

reversed to hazard what would be when wood
was pressed to paper, dreams caught in intaglio.
She drove from Brooklyn through cathedral windows,

past rude stares, to show her prints in "the city,"
smoothing a crumpled New York driver's license,
one of the first earned by a woman, and bearing

four invisible words: "It will be beautiful."
She built no bridge, but crossed this steel
and sand-colored granite arched over schooners

that killed before it joined, that said it's not
just striving, but the risk. With the fixed gaze
of one drawn to hard tasks, she finds me, frowns,

slides into the Ford, and rattles on.
Now, seeing caissons planted in the riverbed,
firm as punctuation, I trek the arch

in wonder. On the Manhattan turnoff,
a road sign reads BRIDGE, white arrow pointing left.
Once you're in that lane, you can't turn back.

HENRY JAMES REVISITING, 1904

Streets "bristle" for me, as when you returned
to lash skyscrapers and cheer the low skylines
of Washington Square. Your bare tribute, "noble,"

to La Farge's painting in Ascension Church,
makes me surmise you were wordless in wonder
at how that tiny chapel could contain

the altarpiece with an American
largeness: lank disciples watch the god soar
until seeing is all they are. You are.

I am. And now I see you struck, then stricken
as you scrawl "doom" in fear of towers to come.
I write to tell you that Ascension stands.

Angels in rows like reeds still sing the flight
high in a brownstone gifted with American
clarity: sun filters through glass saints,

strews roses on the nave, and tells of light
forever, as from fields, not cramped back yards.
It's an American slant on survival.

Tall buildings crowd row houses, not Ascension,
a landmark, *l* for long life. White pear blossoms
fall. Ascension rises. Some things remain:

ailanthus trees that smell of constant summer,
and this church spire, ascended till it's turned,
things being what they are in town, immortal.

THE PAINTINGS OF OUR LIVES

The Annunciation Triptych,
             Robert Campin, the Cloisters

             I

Through leaded windowpanes, the light pours down
less on the holy figures than on objects
waiting to be used, that tell the story:
a fringed towel hung askew, a kettle-laver,

unlit wall sconces, the windblown pages
of a book laid open on a table,
an empty bench the Virgin leans against
as she sits on the floor reading the bible,

not even noticing the angel Gabriel.
Those things, enlarged, furnish the Campin Room,
set here as though a great wave had spewed out
details grown to life-size replicas —

the window, firescreen, candles, gleaming kettle,
an untenanted bench roped off in velvet.
Gathered to fit a corner or a shelf,
those imitations lack the painter's order,

his art of reconciling all that varies:
the red of the Virgin's gown, repeated
in a guard's doublet and in Joseph's tunic,
binds one who sees and one who turns away.

2

Somewhere are the paintings of our lives,
invisible to us — hers, for example,
as she sits fixed on Proust, not looking up.
Across the room, a concert grand piano

once played every day stands quiet now.
It dwarfs her husband's brood of unwound watches,
the marble angel, the Queen Anne chairs,
the porcelain she's never served from, petaled

Tiffany lamps. Unused, the relics shine
like the painter's lily in a jar,
but only while, eyes lit, she says "bronze swan,"
or "jade Buddha," and tells you how it came.

When she gave me a silvery menorah —
one she'd let darken for its vintage glow —
I rubbed it with a cloth, but it went dull
as a shell that's taken from the sea.

I know an elusive master has revealed
her life's design in oils on three wood panels:
a panoply of objects and a gown
the unifying red of her desires.

Last Requests

are clear in books: "Dorset, embrace him...
And make me happy in your unity";
and in old movies: "Take care of my hyacinths."
In opera, last pleas fill the diva's arias.

I've waited for last hopes, my amulets
against silence. My father, dying, spoke
in an urgent Polish he'd not used in years,
but his words, staccato trumpet notes,

were not injunctions. When my mother's life
crested like a wave before it breaks,
I asked her wishes. She said, "Ice cream, quick!"
and hurled a glance that said she was not in pain

but dying, and must hurry on with it.
Lips trembled open: "Don't kiss me again.
No, you catch everything. But thanks for coming."
Then quiet. In a trance, a captive audience,

she could not stop my vows, but not a syllable
I uttered had been left unsaid in tiffs,
snarls at ogres in the stories told
on rainy days until the china mugs

rattled on glass shelves, in alphabet games,
nouns binding us like ropes we strung with beads
and lifted up, verbs spinning like bedsheets
we dried, then pulled taut. Words were for wishing

on first daffodils, secrets kept from others.
Now I'll take any edict, fiat, murmur,
gossip, or prayer. Hers, not another's.
When the phone rang at dawn I thought, wrong number,

and blurred the verdict. Even expecting it,
I was not prepared, nor will I be
in her rooms, tapping a crystal bowl,
waiting for words to burn through it like sun.

One Year Without Mother

1. What Can You Believe?

When your eyes fluttered open, did you think,
searching linden leaves outside your window,
seeing not even me, in that vast blink
of eyes, you would meet God? For sure, I knew

you and mortality: "When I am dead
I want to *be* dead," you insisted, answering
"Priest or rabbi?" questionnaires fusilladed
at you: "One doctor, please." But was there nothing

in all that dark? You held the living fast
and scorned memorials. Your love was here
and now. Like paradise. That now is past.
I ask because I found in your desk drawer

a line you'd copied: "Rejoice in the Lord,"
with "Hear my song" scrawled on the page. Your words.

2. THE PIANO

Once men pried loose a window to haul in
the Knabe grand piano, and I heard
brick scrape dark wood, four legs land with a thud
that shook bare walls. Harsh birth. You played Chopin,

Father tried Brahms as Jacob fought his angel,
and I missed keys. Topaz lamps shone brightly,
never on our sheet music but on family
photographs on the piano: a lost uncle,

decades of cousins. In panic over chords,
I could implore the piano's faces, ponder
the lives it held, or, at the worst times, stare
at statues: Esther, Saint Luke, a clay Buddha.

When the apartment changed hands, I did not
stay to discover how they moved it out.

3. THINGS

Dead? Morning scenes I thought would live: the harbor
you swam, the black-capped bird that grazed your hair,
some steely words I hoped would rust in air.
Dead? Gone to auction: chairs, Regency mirror,

back to the markets where you'd found them. Rings,
a bronze Pegasus, five netsukes, pens
I keep like present moments. Write them down
as painters caught pure light in homely things.

Van Eyck, for instance. Were Virgin and child
all that called him? Or perhaps that miracle
urged him to sanctify a pewter bowl,
amber decanter, figured carpet, tiles

in oils unalterable, clear in the sunlight.
More life to violets, their thisness caught.

4. CEREMONY

To put your house in order, I went back
more than I had to, polished a decanter,
hoisted a painting with your self-stick stuck
behind, "a real Gekko," and scrubbed silver

for unknown others. Needless labor, yet
my privilege: nine women washed Schmuel,
my ancestor, then swaddled him for burial.
A daughter's right. Her rite. How rites persist

when prayer comes hard. My husband's faith, hard-won,
is only that the genome project may
restore the sick. But last year, at the cemetery,
I watched him twist a shovel spade-side down
in a half-remembered ritual, and then
dig it in earth he scattered on your coffin.

5. WORDS IN THE DARK

Seeking clues to you, I lit wall domes,
probed angels, and unlocked a rosewood case
of gods, saw mirrors throw back rooms in rooms,
but no image. Then, in a darker place,

I found a crowded album with one photo
of you in plaid, resting on one elbow,
with one hand on a book. You'd seen Keats so,
perhaps. I caught you then in shadow:

shirts jammed in closets, rouge for evening looks.
Dad strode, you slithered. Somehow it was fine.
But in your desk were words: on cards, in diaries,
on envelopes, on stained flyleaves of books,
your handwriting, like links of massed gold chains
binding your thoughts that struggled to be free.

6. Ring Sale

Years past, you opened your hand on a diamond,
stone side in, blinking in traffic lights.
I could not keep it. I'd have lost the band
family collectors locked in cabinets

for centuries, their pledge to a new world.
You said Grandma displayed the ring at dinners,
not when she painted, chopped herbs in a bowl,
or scooped earth to sink roots. With bare fingers

you sipped vermouth. But that day, at the store,
you wondered if the setting would be altered —
art deco, silver violets circling light —
your eyes imploring me to want the diamond,
blessed with more life. I had just one regret:
I'd not inherited your tiny hand.

7. EAGLE

Those tales you called back: how you nudged a door
and found the Hebrew poet in your room —
the couch was made for you, your bed for visitors.
Standing, eyes raised, the man declaimed a poem

about an eagle's shadow on a mountain:
Look there! It wavers as the bird looks down
and watches watches watches. You were ten
and lacked the meaning, but you heard the tones,

not of prayers but curses, bells, wings' rush,
saw him hunched over, and cried, "Eagle Angel."
The story over, I saw, in that hush,
a shadow veil your eyes as though the eagle
had flown over them. How could I tell you then
I'd heard those wings flapping in terrible silence?

8. The Fall

I see you as you spiraled, steps to pavement,
then stood, unharmed, saying you knew the way
to fall. You sprinted on and changed the subject,
dodging remarks about your leaf-ballet.

When you were hurled into a lake at three
to learn hard strokes, you splashed and rose a swimmer,
master of surfacing. Down with disease,
you bobbed, gasped air, and whirled away from danger.

I heard in the clack-clack of your stride
keys that typed freedom, and I lagged at your side.
Would you trick death? On a steep bluff one day,
you tossed a fallen beach rose to the sea.
Months later, the earth opened and I knew
where you would go at last I could not follow.

9. Keeper

Objects heaped end to end in the mind's basement:
Dad's English passport inscribed "Borosowa,"
probably "Warsaw," misheard; travel posters;
a diamond band broken into three crescents;

Grandmother's 1920s driver's license;
a photo montage, faces without names;
embroidered table linens; a bronze lamb
that can't be kept *or* lost. I dread that basement,

where chairs are slung from nails or stacked on tables.
Like script on sand-covered stones, my mind's images
would answer everything, but in secret languages.
I yearn to brave dank stairs and touch them all,
but there's no space to turn. Cart them away?
No, shut the iron door and tell the story.

10. A Goldsmith in His Shop

God lives in the detail. When Petrus Christus
painted a goldsmith's shop with coral, rubies,
gold rings, and a glass jar with God-sent clarity,
perhaps he meant the smith to be Eligius,

the patron saint of guilds, a weighted balance,
the Last Judgment. In any case, those figures
have had, and will have, rays beyond the artist
and subjects: the smith, street-smart, self-assured,

a couple to be wed, the woman eager
to touch the band, eyes low, her rich brocades,
though ostentatious, hallowed as the wall
of shelves cluttered with beads and silver pitchers.
Base objects were examined from all sides
until they shone. *God lives in the detail.*

11. The Lesson of a Tree

"I dreamed I died and woke in Central Park,"
you said one year ago, green lawns and puffy
maples before you. Spring is back. White pear trees
tiptoe expectantly, like brides. Deep pink

azaleas soon will shock an urban garden
without your wonder. You'd see roses grow
uncut, as though you knew you could not own
them. Once, when we lived just beyond the skyline

that bounds the park, I called that first home mine.
Now as the days float past like a cloud's dragon
that changes to a sparrow, I discover
moments: veins on a leaf, bands on a plover.

Perhaps you're in the world Li Po imagined
that we aspire to but never own.

12. LAMENTATION SCENE

Greek red-figured vase, fifth century B.C.

All loss is painted here in this dead beauty
set on carved wood. Thin lips fixed in a smile,
moon-slivers of shut eyes, have shown for centuries
of wars what peace is. But her man's not tranquil,

calling her back, hands open on the bier,
head bowed, eyes wide, mouth twisted in his grief,
nor is the young woman who claws her hair
over the poised dead, turbulent in life.

After this peak, the proud matron will fade
even as Achilles, mourning his fall,
would slave on earth rather than rule the dead.
Her afterlife: those hands that reach, that pull;
silence but for the words: *Memoire.*
In memory. *Mnemosyne. Zakhor.*

13. OFFERING

You said: "Driven from homes in the pogroms,
women took only their brass candelabra
for Sabbath lights." You never kindled them,
but kept a pair because their reedy limbs

promised to dance in flame. Dying, you yearned
for light to read by, to see roses burn
in a white bowl, to see what life was left.
I give you now June bugs, a sunlit leaf,

snowfalls in slanted lines, a great white egret's
scarflike wing flaps, and I laugh with your laughter
at amber lamps that shone but seldom lit
the page, harsh neon signs that winked at night.
I give you metaphor in place of prayer:
May you hear "Let there be light!" where there's light.

14. Credo

Some nights I wonder why I juxtapose
brass lamps that hold our flame with a high mass,
Rogier's Madonna lilies in a vase
with Tai Chin's river hand-scroll. I suppose,

as sun glints off a stone monk in half-lotus
and buffs metal, that when mother and daughter,
tradition-proud, saw death, they kept one ruler
while learning other holy truths. Though trust

came slow, God governed language. "Go fight God,"
you said, and I surmised death calls for images
odd as a black skimmer's white underside,
souls locked in pines, angels that fly in V's.
Hosannas, kaddish, Oms, sing on my pages,
hold back the dark, help me live out my days.

15. REQUIEM

Hear *Tuba mirum spargens sonum.* Hear
trombones, brass, woodwinds, and the chorus raise
visions of trumpetblare on Judgment Day.
I see the dead turn, Mozart's fear my fear,

and wish that his salvation had been stirred
by salve: "I'm justa goin' over home,"
blessings, or simply *Requiem aeternum.*
Lord, give them rest. Stop there. Perhaps those words

of terror woke his noble cadences
and heightened softer passages to come.
Maybe they set free rage; before deliverance
verses came, he would die. But in that storm,
I thought I heard a phrase stab like a knife
and echo, unsung, uninscribed: Praise life.

NEW POEMS

Repentance of an Art Critic, 1925

"Existe-t-il une peinture juive?"
—Fritz Vanderpyl

Some learned the palette is the devil's platter,
the brush a crucifix: by law, no icons,
no graven images "made unto thee."

Yet Soutine dries creeds in the Paris sun,
his strokes prayers for pardon. Others are freer.
A mystery. I find no common style,

no *ism,* nest for thought, as in a pen stand.
Marc Chagall's villages, Soutine's dead turkeys,
Sonia Delauney's rings, make an odd stew.

In Kisling's painting, Kiki of Montparnasse
lies on flowered silk. Nearby, a window opens
on more windows. Air, light. Still I say,

could Michelangelo have carved *La Pietà*
without belief, his trust only in stone?
Even Rouault, godless, hunted by God,

painted Christ's head slashed with lines. How faith crushes
and builds. But not them. Torn up from dry soil,
replanted, pruned back, they blossom again

like horse chestnuts under a new god.
Their only faith, if one can call it that,
lurks in this day's sunlit buildings, leaves

that still sparkle with raindrops, and brushstrokes
that catch the glimmer. Some fled pogroms.
But take Modigliani, from Livorno,

Whose women, swans, gaze with clouded pupils.
The painter's stare. Doorlocks pried open,
they blink under puff-clouded skies,

talk at Le Dôme until the paint runs free,
then, each to his easel, gather beliefs
like lilies that die as the canvas blooms.

Can the most foreign of the new Parisians
share anything besides a lost law?
I've said no. Was I wrong? I ask Kisling,

who waves at his painting. It seizes me,
and a voice rises from so deep I know
it cannot be my own: the sheer exactness

of bowl, knife, apple, keeps us from loss
by capturing the day that does not end.
In Kisling's vision of his studio,

two forms stand at either end of a table:
within the oil is his oil of a nude
darting furtive glances, and Modigliani's

long head. Between them are paintbrushes
poised like rockets waiting to explode,
a pipe, a half-filled glass, and a hand of cards.

Flags

Red, yellow banners on sloops in the bay
catch the erratic wind; each with one pattern,
distinct, indelible, soars like a phrase
heard once that resounds over the waves' din.

My father stood without a flag in silence,
an advertising man, stunned when his client,
a mill owner, routinely called the carders
of color, or of foreign birth, "those others."

Once, called to the silver-and-gilt table
where custom had a dinner guest say grace,
his turn came. With crushed rage he knew
he'd passed, "A" for "Accepted." Speech came slow

when he tried to say, "You will drown in lies."
Instead, he lifted a white handkerchief,
knotted the corners, clapped it to his head,
and chanted, *Baruch atah Adonai* . . .

to a startled host. Now I hear his prayer
that's printed in bold letters on a handkerchief
among red, yellow flags beyond the wharf,
as I grope for words in the mist-thick air.

1932

All I have of the last visit to Germany,
my father keen to show his New World bride,
is this photo: a sleek lad and his father
are sentinels; each man clutches a chair,

arms flexed to hold up beams of a falling house.
My mother bends to curb lank arms and legs
that trail generations of New York and Kansas.
Dad's mother has a farmer's mottled hands,

skin pleated by the sun. With set jaw, wordless,
she had begged them to stay; there would be peace.
The photo is stamped DANZIG, city of change:
now Germany, now Poland, now between,

and that year what Dad called safe on first.
To Warsaw, his past, he dared not return.
My mother is younger than I am now.
She was always young. In Berlin, she had guessed

people wore armbands with Vedic signs
to show that they were blind. In this split second,
long fingers stroke her mother-in-law's shoulder
as if to skim a lake. My mother stares

with her elder's eyes at the camera lens.
Dad's sisters, home from college, glance away.
One would be shot to death, another beaten.
But my mother is Ruth in a knitted suit,

who vows to a farmhand in a peasant blouse:
Whither thou goest I will go. Where thou diest . . .
Now on my lawn I cry: Don't stay in Germany!
Come back on the last ship. Let me be born.

Jewish Cemetery, Eleventh Street

This is no place for death. No rangy weeds,
no leafy trees. No long drive to a meadow.
There's nothing like an urban cemetery,
stuck between buildings, students loping by,

to teach us all the measure of our days.
Today a walker whistles by the graveyard.
A shopper leans a bag against the gate
and hunts names through black spikes: one, ISAAC HARBY,

d. 1838, is blurred on stone.
I looked him up. He was a translator
of Hebrew prayers many would save unaltered.
Biographies that tell all reveal nothing,

but I know Harby dug for English words
like quartz to cut and polish until they glistened.
Dying, he read the psalms out loud to friends.
I think the line that came with his last breath

must have been *For thou, Lord, hast made me glad,*
words that danced on. A spectral Isaac Harby
who caught art-talk next door, site of the Grapevine,
now leaps to current titles at the cinema

and blesses the tomb-seer in agate phrases.
I bend to scoop up pebbles for his grave
and rattle the locked gate. When I walk on,
faces beam out at me, restless as verbs.

JOB'S QUESTION ON NEVIS

"Turn back!" was all she snapped out as she passed
in a red dress that caught sunrays through mist.
I saw her lurch upwind, kick off spiked heels,
climb out to the edge of a knife-sharp rockpile,

and, arms outstretched, lead the sea's tympani,
lure the din, guiding the steamy waves
to shore. *Will the Almighty answer me?*
she sang out to the ocean's rising octaves,

as blown palms pointed scarflike fronds to land.
Earlier that Sunday, she had prayed
to a black Christ in a church on the island,
droned verses for a safe calm, and trekked homeward

to board white louvered windows for the storm.
She had refused the chapel's sanctuary
to ask the ocean why the wind ripped homes
and would again. Her anger captured me,

and stayed when I saw rain gleam on red ginger,
drench trumpets islanders call yellow-bells,
and soak ixora. Bonelike bits of shells
and conchs lay on the beach as on an altar.

Silent, I watched her. Under a blank sky,
where waves broke over coral, in thick haze,
pitched forward to hear the whirlwind's reply,
she shook a fist, then opened hands in praise.

LONG WINTER DUSK

No ordinary dusk. The sun
sank in a blaze of steel chimneys.
A man's lean shadow faded, then
the man himself. My words gone dry,

I searched for sidewalk chips, for stars,
for streetlamps, and for any bit
or slice or shred of all there was
before it flamed to ash at sunset.

No elm's bent twigs, no watertanks
above me, I groped for a plane tree,
no longer there. After that blank,
there was light: electricity.

Bright windows in bare offices
of buildings that had been eyeless
shone in neon epiphanies
above leftover Christmas lights.

I never spoke of how I saw
the void and how I saw it end
as in a room at Tiffany's,
the studio where formless lampstands

waited for the glassmaker
to turn glass into peonies,
wisteria, seas, dragonflies
of light. And light was everywhere.

GRANDMOTHER'S SEA

roars in my closet, oil on wood, gilt frame.
"This was your birthplace. Yes, Bensonhurst, Brooklyn.

Before subways, the ocean hissed on sand
and bluefish leaped at sunrise." Her deep voice

gathered force like sea waves. Outside the window,
a gas-tank truck rattled down her syllables

and groaned at a neighbor's door. In the painting
a woman stood, wind-tousled, with a basket

of plums on a brief panhandle of shore,
gazing at water. Except for her blue apron,

brushstrokes were murky—auburn dress, mud sky.
My grandmother wore white embroidered shirtwaists

when she stirred iron pots and tended roses.
One day I dabbed the painting with a cloth.

Dust gone, the drab seawater shone cerulean.
On shore an egret was a blazing question,

its yellow bill a penpoint under skies
of prophetic light. A tern hovered so close

to cliffs so sharp that fish stench filled the air.
Under backing, words loomed, scratched on wood:

"Ellen Terry starring in *The Good Hope*."
Artist's name blurred. Not Brooklyn. Still I know

that even after subways came, the sea
rasped outside the garden of my first house.

STEPS

"And down and down and down,"
the toddler's mother sings
as he clears every ledge.

Midway we cross their path.
In rain, the museum's steps
loom like the Giant's Stairway

to Guardi's Ducal Palace.
"And up and up and up"
is what I do not say

as you stagger for balance.
Once I'd scaled that summit,
hunted over the crowd,

and saw you below, holding
two hot dogs and white roses;
you vaulted, took the steps

two at a time, then three,
and leaped to where we met.
Your smile is broader now.

You see more. On this day
of wavering, we hear
a Triton blow the horn

where Giotto's Magi open
hands that rise in air:
up, and up, and up.

BITTER SPRING

Breaking winter's lock,
crocuses knife upward
through hard ground.

Tulips bend in wind—
lucid, red-orange,
fired to blare.

Iced magnolia branches
raise up white-pink fists.
It's their time,

though my breath is steam.
Under lime-green trees,
in late sun,

the park's comeback in color,
the blank face of a child
still alone.

An Empty Surfboard on a Quiet Sea

will always gleam in sunlight. There it is,
paint chipped off, still afloat. It calls to mind
the day a man strode out in gale-force winds
and dense fog. He straddled a slab like this,

lay prone on green wood, rose up on one knee,
arms flailing, stood, and walked high waves to shore.
On land, he stroked his wetsuit, slicked back hair,
kissed the plank for luck, then turned to sea.

As the surfer hauled it, he and the board
were one, a tall cross for a gravestone marker.
I shouted, "Stop!" as though he were no stranger.
He vanished and raced back. I shook in fear

for us who risk the breaker's ride and fall,
or skid to firm sand and survive the gale.

NOTES

BURN DOWN THE ICONS

"Surely as Certainty Changes":
> stanza 3, line 2, "And proteolysis, 'the end of
> change/Changing in the end'": The term designates the
> enzymatic process by which protein is broken down.

"The Other Side of Humankind":
> Countess Catherine Karolyi's husband, Michel, was the
> first president of the Hungarian Republic. In Paris, she
> was a correspondent for *Life* and wrote for other jour-
> nals in English, French, and German. Exiled from her
> home in Hungary, she invited to her villa in Vence
> artists from five continents, sometimes pairing residents
> of Western countries with those who lived under Com-
> munist rule.

"Spain, 1964":
> This poem was previously published under the title "In
> the Police State."

"Letter to Helen":
> Helena Waldman-Gold, my father's sister, was a practic-
> ing pediatrician who declined to leave Warsaw even af-
> ter the Nazi harassment of Jews in the 1930s. When
> World War II ended, my family learned that she had
> died in the Warsaw ghetto uprising in 1943. An
> Auschwitz survivor reported that Helen, believing she
> would be deported to a concentration camp, had

climbed the tower of a municipal building, run to the ledge, pulled down the Polish flag from its staff, and ripped the flag to shreds. She stood for a while, holding the red cloth, before she was shot down by a Nazi guard. After speaking with the survivor, my aunt Beta wrote from Israel, "It was an act of revenge on the Poles for having given her away."

      Section 2, line 10: "Awakening at last..." In Seneca's *Hercules Furens*, Hercules awakens to find he has committed murder in a fit of madness. Refusing to place blame on a god, he accepts responsibility.

HEMISPHERES

"Sutton Hoo Ship Burial":
      For the description of the ship and its excavation, I relied on *The Sutton Hoo Ship Burial*, by Rupert Bruce-Mitford (British Museum Publications, 1979). The burial mounds lay on the estate of Edith May Pretty, who led the search for the Sutton Hoo treasures.

"Instructions for a Journey":
      "God commanded Metatron, the Angel of the Face, to conduct Moses to the celestial regions amid the sound of music and song."—*Gedullet Mosheh*

FOR THAT DAY ONLY

"Footsteps on Lower Broadway":
      line 12: "I ... headed for Pfaff's." Pfaff's Café. Charles Pfaff, owner; established 1856. In an interview, Whitman was quoted as having said, "I used to go to Pfaff's every night" (*Brooklyn Daily Eagle*, 11 July 1866).

Stanza 4, lines 40 through 50: In March 1842, Whitman attended services twice at the Shearith Israel Synagogue on Crosby Street, between Spring and Broome, in lower Manhattan. Recounting both visits in the *Aurora* (March 28–29), Whitman wrote, "The heart within us felt awed as in the presence of memorials from an age that had passed away centuries ago. The strange and discordant tongue—the mystery, and all the associations that crowded themselves in troops upon our mind—made a thrilling sensation to creep through every nerve." Although Whitman does not refer to Judaism in his great poetic passages concerning world religions, he does incorporate Hebrew rhythms and imagery in his verse. Apparently the impact of Jewish ritual was deeper than he had supposed.

"Urban Bestiary":
This poem appeared earlier as "Stone Demons" in a sequence called "Bestiaries."

"Julian of Norwich":
Julian was a fourteenth-century anchorite who took her name from the parish church of St. Julian in Conisford at Norwich, an East Anglia town. "From a window in her cell she could view the Eucharist and from another window she could assist people seeking spiritual counsel"—*What Is Anglicanism?*, by Urban T. Holmes III (Morehouse-Barlow, 1982).

"Rescue in Pescallo":
According to local tales, the statue of Christ in the Church of San Giacomo was found washed up on the lakeshore. The details here are entirely fictional.

"Eve's Unnaming":

> The idea for this poem was suggested by Harold Bloom, in *The Western Canon.* He quotes Ursula K. Le Guin, who writes in "She Unnames Them," in *Buffalo Gals and Other Animal Presences* (Capra, 1987), "Most of them accepted namelessness with the perfect indifference with which they had accepted and ignored their names."

"Chaim Soutine":

> My information is culled from *Soutine,* by Monroe Wheeler (Metropolitan Museum of Art, 1950), and from the author, to whom I am grateful for this and much more.

"Poem Ending with a Phrase from the Psalms":

> Psalm 90, line 12.

"Blue Dawn":

> For Alexandra Paschen Brainerd.

"Storm Watch":

> The Frederick Turner painting referred to here is *Snowstorm: Steamboat off a harbour's mouth making signals in shallow water, and going by the lead* (1840). According to Lawrence Gowing's *Turner: Imagination and Reality* (Museum of Modern Art, 1966), Turner said, "I got the sailors to lash me to the mast to observe it; I was lashed for four hours, and I did not expect to escape, but I felt bound to record it if I did." Although a plaque in the National Gallery, London, questions the existence of a

ship named *Ariel* operating out of Harwich, Turner's account remains vivid in my mind.

"Black and White":

Paul Celan, born Paul Ancel in Romanian Boukovina in 1920, survived Nazi forced labor camps and died a suicide in Paris, in 1970. For information about his early years, I relied on *Paul Celan: A Biography of his Youth,* by Israel Chalfen (Persea, 1991).

"Margaret Fuller":

Margaret Fuller drowned when her ship, the *Elizabeth,* struck the sands off Fire Island in 1850. With her were her husband, the marchese Giovanni Angelo Ossoli, and their child. Born in Boston in 1810, Fuller traveled to Italy in 1847, where she supported the revolution of the Roman Republic and wrote about it for the *New York Tribune.* I came upon the story of Fuller and the *Elizabeth* in Walt Whitman's notes about Long Island shipwrecks collected in *Specimen Days.* My information is gathered from the *Memoirs of Margaret Fuller Ossoli* (Phillips, Sampson, 1852) and from Paula Blanchard's *Margaret Fuller* (Delacorte/Sam Lawrence, 1978).

"Brooklyn Bridge":

Details about the bridge are from Alan Trachtenberg's *Brooklyn Bridge: Fact and Symbol* (Oxford University Press, 1965).

"The Paintings of Our Lives":

The Annunciation Altarpiece (c. 1425) by Robert Campin, the Flemish master, is also known as *The Annunciation Triptych, The Merode Altarpiece,* and *Robert*

Campin's Triptych. It hangs in the Cloisters, in New York, where it is called *The Annunciation Triptych.*

"Last Requests":
"Dorset, embrace him" is from Shakespeare's *Richard III,* act II, scene i.

"One Year Without Mother"
"What Can You Believe?":
"Rejoice in the Lord" refers here to Psalm 33, line 1.
"Things":
Jan van Eyck, *The Virgin and Child* (c. 1425), oil on wood.
"A Goldsmith in His Shop":
The origin of the phrase "God lives in the detail" is uncertain, although Flaubert is believed to have said, "Le bon Dieu est dans le détail," and according to E. H. Gombrich, Aby Warburg wrote, "Der liebe Gott steckt im Detail" ("God dwells in minutiae"). The painting by Petrus Christus, *A Goldsmith in His Shop, Possibly Saint Eligius,* is at the Metropolitan Museum of Art, New York.
"Credo":
"Rogier's Madonna lilies" refers to *The Annunciation,* by Rogier van der Weyden, at the Metropolitan Museum of Art, New York. Tai Chin's hand-scroll, "Fishermen on the River," is at the Freer Gallery of Art, Washington, D.C. I found that and other hand-scrolls reprinted handsomely in *Endless River: Li Po and Tu Fu, a Friendship in Poetry,* translated and edited by Sam Hamill (Weatherhill, 1993).

"Repentance of an Art Critic":

"Existe-t-il une peinture juive?" ("Is there a Jewish paint-
ing style?") — In 1925, an article of that title by Fritz
Vanderpyl appeared in *Mercure de France,* a Paris re-
view. Vanderpyl asked, "Where did it come from, and so
suddenly, this desire to paint on the part of these de-
scendants of the twelve tribes, this passion for paint-
brush and palette, which — in spite of the Law — is be-
ing tolerated, even encouraged, in the most orthodox
circles?" The poem was inspired by "Paris in New York:
French Jewish Artists in Private Collections," an exhibit
at the Jewish Museum.

"Jewish Cemetery, Eleventh Street":

Second cemetery of the Spanish and Portuguese Syna-
gogue, Shearith-Israel, 11th Street near Sixth Avenue.
Founded in 1805, the burial ground was cut through in
1830, and only a wedge remains. Built in 1838, the
Grapevine was a roadhouse frequented by artists.

"An Empty Surfboard on a Quiet Sea":

This appeared as "An Empty Surfboard on a Flat Sea" in
the *Paris Review,* which asked a number of writers to
compose poems bearing that title.

GRACE SCHULMAN has received the Aiken Taylor Award for Modern American Poetry, New York University's Delmore Schwartz Award for Poetry, and a poetry fellowship from the New York Foundation of the Arts. Her poetry has received two Pushcart Prizes and has been anthologized in *The Best American Poetry* and *The Best of the Best American Poetry, 1988–1998*. Schulman is Distinguished Professor of English at Baruch College, City University of New York, as well as the poetry editor of *The Nation* and a former director of the Poetry Center of the 92nd Street Y. She lives in New York City.